Manifestations
of Male Image
in the World's Cultures

Manifestations of Male Image in the World's Cultures

Edited by
Renata Iwicka

Jagiellonian University Press

Series: Bezkresy Kultury / The Vastness of Culture

With the financial support of the Centre for Comparative Studies in Civilisations at the Jagiellonian University in Kraków

REVIEWER
dr hab. Paweł Tański, prof. UMK

COVER DESIGN
Sebastian Wojnowski
Cover photo: *Male Nude* (1880) by Gustav Klimt. Original from The Art Institute of Chicago. Digitally enhanced by rawpixel

ISBN 978-83-233-5043-9
ISBN 978-83-233-7273-8 (e-book)

JAGIELLONIAN
UNIVERSITY
PRESS

www.wuj.pl

Jagiellonian University Press
Editorial Offices: Michałowskiego 9/2, 31-126 Kraków
Phone: +48 12 663 23 80
Distribution: Phone: +48 12 631 01 97
Cell Phone: +48 506 006 674, e-mail: sprzedaz@wuj.pl
Bank: PEKAO SA, IBAN PL 80 1240 4722 1111 0000 4856 3325

CONTENTS

RENATA IWICKA
ⓘ http://orcid.org/0000-0001-6554-8841

PREFACE

The main goal of this book is to add into the growing field of Masculinity Studies the multifaceted reflection on the theme of "maleness" viewed from vastly different perspectives. The volume offers a wide range of perspectives, starting from the Antiquity and ending with the newest trends in religious movements, or characters in the television shows.

The articles in the volume are presented in the alphabetical order, according to their titles. There is in total 8 texts, carefully chosen for their variety in proposed perspectives and methodology. In this short presentation I will refrain from using the titles of the Authors, so that everyone would be treated with the same attitude and respect.

The opening text takes the research to Japan of the 11th century and builds a bridge between the ideals of the apogee of the aristocrat culture, and contemporary re-examining of the ideal male. In *"A Jewel beyond Compare": Prince Hikaru Genji as a Perfect Male of the Heian Period in the Light of Popular Culture Theories*, Anna Kuchta and Joanna Malita-Król apply the theories of the popular culture to the text written a millennium ago and prove that such interpretation gives new life to, seemingly, overexamined work of literature.

In the second text, *Cicero and Male Virtue*, Katarzyna Borkowska describes how Cicero attempted to reinvent Roman concept of *virtus*, so that his interests (Greek culture seen as the sign of feminisation) and himself would be placed firmly in the "maleness" category.

Third text leaves the Antiquity and European continent to examine the masculinity concept within the discourse regarding Native Americans and settlers. In *Kill the Savage, Save the Man – James Welch's Chronicle of Native American History*, Agnieszka Gondor-Wiercioch presents the process of destroying the stereotype of a Native American male as, to borrow the Author's own words, "Savage Warrior of the Plains." Such rare theme and deep analysis of Welch's literary work prove that shattering the stereotypes is a long, but sometimes necessary process.

With the fourth text, the focus moves to the increasingly popular within a scientific community region – to Afghanistan. In *On (Self-)Representations of Masculinity in Siyāmak Herawi's Short Stories*, Khalil A. Arab and Mateusz M. Kłagisz examine the masculinity within the frame of the Muslim world, using short stories as the primary texts of their reflection. Such research adds tremendously to the vast amount of social and cultural issues examined within Islamic studies, but also – by comparison – to general studies.

Next article brings the theme of "maleness" almost to its emblematic representation. In *Power, Masculinity, and War: Superman, a Case Study*, Kwasu David Tembo examines the character of Superman, who not only embodies the "American values," but also serves as the starting point in representing the ideal male (an unattainable goal for most, given Superman's out-of-this-Earth provenance), moving through various embodiments and changes. Close reading of the character, along with the concepts of masculinity and Otherness open new possibilities in understanding such well known character.

In *Korean Television Drama Series*, Author examines recent changes in portraying the male lead in Korean television series (Kdramas). Within the span of few years only, the typical male lead changed from being a dominating, often cold and haughty character, to more empathetic and warm. This trend goes against the growing misogynistic voices heard from various generations, however the power of television may create a new model, attractive to those who do not have to prove their masculinity.

Next article takes the narrative to the supernatural dominion. In *Stripping the Vampire. Erotic Imaginations and Sexual Fantasies in Paranormal Romances (a Study of Selected Examples)*, Ksenia Olkusz presents deep insight into the transformation of the titular vampire – from the terrifying monster to the beautiful undead, worthy of desire and adoration. Sometimes, the re-imagining of this creature even borders on pornography. This shift is skillfully explained using various literary sources as the primary texts of the research.

The last article changes the point of research completely – in *The Horned God: Divine Male Principle in British Traditional Wicca*, Joanna Malita-Król examines the portrayal of one half of the Wiccan godly duo – that is of the God who plays the active role as the fertilising aspect of the two. Author analyses the image of the God in his four avatars: "mainly the Horned One, but also Lord of Death, Oak and Holly King, Green Man" (to borrow the Author's own words). This deep insight into the Wiccan community is definitely a much-needed addition to the masculinity studies, as it can have an effect on society and culture.

From the prairies of America through Afghanistan and finally landing in Japan – the range of the articles proves that the reflection on ever-changing constructs of masculinity is something worth exploring, using various methodological lenses and focal points.

ACKNOWLEDGMENTS

This book would not be possible if it were not for the help of many people involved in this long and tenuous project. First of all – Authors, who showed amazing, noteworthy patience. Professor Marta Kudelska who gave this publication a green light and made it possible to be shown to the world. Individual reviewers, and of course Professor Paweł Tański as a final and amazing reviewer, who recommended this book to be published. All proofreaders and editors, those who read the final versions of the articles and corrected them, advisors like Kimmie White, Dr. Lidia Grzybowska whose suggestions only added more insight into the texts. Very deep gratitude must be expressed towards Mrs. Dorota Kawala, who has shown incredible patience and leniency towards the writer of these words.

And of course, I thank Kim Jonghyeon, whose voice helped me navigate through difficult times while working on this volume.

ANNA KUCHTA
ⓘ http://orcid.org/0000-0001-7841-0198

JOANNA MALITA-KRÓL
ⓘ http://orcid.org/0000-0002-7668-5902

"A JEWEL BEYOND COMPARE": PRINCE HIKARU GENJI AS A PERFECT MALE OF THE HEIAN PERIOD IN THE LIGHT OF POPULAR CULTURE THEORIES

Abstract: *The Tale of Genji* was written in the Heian period at the beginning of the 11th century by Murasaki Shikibu. The authoress, herself a lady of the Empress' court, depicted an ideal hero – Prince Hikaru Genji – who later became a perfect male for other court ladies. This paper analyses how Genji is presented in the novel and how he was received by the readers. The main research perspective combines analysis of the text itself along with pop-culture theories (referencing, among others, Haruo Shirane, Dominic Strinati and Henry Jenkins). With such methodology, we aim to show Prince Genji within a broad perspective of Japanese culture.

Keywords: Hikaru Genji, The Tale of Genji, Murasaki Shikibu, popular culture, Heian

INTRODUCTION ■

It was already Yasunari Kawabata,[1] who said that "*The Tale of Genji* in particular is the highest pinnacle of Japanese literature. Even down to our day there has not been a piece of fiction to compare with it. That such a modern work should have been written in the 11th century is a miracle,

---

[1] For the transcript of the Japanese words and names, the Hepburn romanisation system is used. Japanese names are given in the Western order (with personal name first and family name second).

and as a miracle the work is widely known abroad."[2] The aim of this paper is to present and analyse the portrait of the main protagonist of *The Tale of Genji* by Murasaki Shikibu (c. 978–c. 1026). *The Tale of Genji* (*Genji monogatari*, Jpn. 源氏物語[3]) is often considered to be the first novel in the world,[4] but it also remains a particularly abundant source of knowledge about the Heian period (794–1185), during which it came into existence. The novel concentrates on the character of Prince Hikaru Genji (also called "The Shining Prince", Japanese *hikaru*, 光る, means "to shine"), the son of the Emperor and the most flawless hero of all. It tells the story of his life – filled with numerous affairs – and also depicts the customs of aristocracy of the Heian period within political and sociological context (especially intrigues at the court) with remarkable descriptive realism.

In this paper we will present Genji as a popular culture hero and analyse not only the novel in which he appears for the first time, but also other texts from Heian period, as we intend to trace the reception of the protagonist in social and cultural context. Such a perspective allows us to grasp the very core of the "Genji culture"[5] as we aim to study Prince Genji not only as a character from the novel, but as a phenomenon of Japanese culture. While we do not aim to prove that *The Tale of Genji* functions exactly as modern works of pop culture;[6] we believe that the characteristics and socio-cultural reception of the novel and its hero since 11th century indicate their pop-cultural character. Therefore, applying new methodologies to historical works and comparing them with modern ones creates an innovative and fresh perspective which may lead to a better understanding of Prince Genji and his tale.

1. HEIAN CONTEXT: GENJI IS BORN

The Tale of Genji was written by lady Murasaki Shikibu (a lady-in-waiting at the Imperial Court of the empress Shōshi[7]) in Heian Japan – a peri-

---

[2]   Y. Kawabata, *Nobel Lecture* [www 01].

[3]   As the aim of the presented article is not a linguistic analysis of *The Tale of Genji*, Edward Seindensticker's English translation of the novel is used as a main source material.

[4]   Cf. H. Shirane, The Tale of Genji *and the Dynamics of Cultural Production*, p. 1.

[5]   Ibidem, p. 1.

[6]   In the paper, the terms "pop-culture" and "popular culture" are used interchangeably.

[7]   Fujiwara no Shōshi, who was the wife of the Emperor Ichijō and the Empress of Japan from c. 1000 to c. 1011.

od of almost undisturbed inner peace and tranquillity (reflected in the era name itself), prosperity and aristocratic rule, both politically and culturally. While the real power was in the hands of the Fujiwara clan, the Imperial Court – depicted also in Lady Murasaki's[8] work – served as a birthplace of sublime culture. Aristocrats gathered in capital city, Heian-kyō (today's Kyōto) and devoted themselves to poetry (*waka*), dance, music, calligraphy and other cultural activities. The authoress herself, as many noble women of the Heian period, spent her time at the court writing (aside from *The Tale of Genji*, the most prominent example of *monogatari* genre, her poetry and diaries survived to our times as well), focusing her novel on what she knew best: every-day life of aristocrats – from courtly romances to political intrigues. "She certainly had time to record what was going on,"[9] points Richard Bowring, as he imagines that Lady Murasaki "tended to remain aloof, observing court ceremonial from a distance."[10] It is worth stating that Lady Murasaki covers the life in the Heian period so thoroughly, that even nowadays *The Tale of Genji* remains one of the main sources of knowledge about Heian culture (e.g. Heian music[11]). As a true classic, *The Tale of Genji* is therefore "rooted in the climate and history of a particular country"[12] but "widely appreciated, transcending time and place."[13]

The culture of the Heian period, created almost exclusively by aristocrats and for aristocrats (although folk culture must have been present as well, it had no impact on nobility and we can barely trace it nowadays), existed within strict rules of aesthetics:

> In the Heian court of that time there was abroad a spirit which was probably more purely aesthetic than any that can be found anywhere in the world at any other period of history. That spirit was an aestheticism that was something more than a pose, something more than a cult, something

---

8 As pointed by J. M. Maki, "Lady Murasaki" is the most common and accepted English translation of the authoress pseudonym, which is why this is how we will refer to her in this article (to avoid confusion, Murasaki – the character from the novel – will be referred to simply as "Murasaki"). Cf. J. M. Maki, *Lady Murasaki and* The Genji Monogatari, p. 481.

9 R. Bowring, op. cit., p. 4.

10 Ibidem.

11 Cf. R. Garfias, *Music of a Thousand Autumns: The Tōgaku Style of Japanese Court Music*, pp. 22–23.

12 M. Emmerich, The Tale of Genji: *Translation, Canonization, and World Literature*, p. 16.

13 Ibidem.

more than a philosophy, something more than refinement for refinement's sake, something more than we can re-create even in our imaginations in this twentieth century.[14]

Therefore, while noble people of Heian were urged to create (good knowledge and skilful usage of literary classics was expected from any noblemen while exchanging poems was an obligatory part of courtship and important addition in everyday conversations), their creative freedom was limited. *The Tale of Genji* is no exception to this rule – being a *monogatari* (Jpn. 物語, meaning "tale" or "narrative"), Lady Murasaki's work fits well within the peak of the very genre popularity, making her novel easy understandable by the readers. In most general terms, a Heian period *monogatari* was a narrative tale depicting a fictional story (sometimes partly inspired by historical events or people) and filled with numerous poems (mainly *tanka*, "short poem" consisting of five units), as it was poetry rather than prose that was considered the most important form of literature of the Heian period. While the genre of *monogatari* has many sub-genres, *tsukuri monogatari* (aristocratic court romance) has its origin in the storytelling of women, which impacted both the content of such novels and their form. While educated men of Heian wrote their literary works in Chinese, women – who did not need to prove their fluency in Chinese to be respected as writers (and members of noble society) – used the Japanese language, developing their own sub-genre of Japanese prose. Lady Murasaki, despite being well-educated in Chinese classics (a trait rather unusual for a Heian lady-in-waiting), decided to write the story of the Shining Prince in Japanese as well, therefore appointing fellow court ladies as her model readers.[15]

The Tale of Genji consists of 54 chapters that portray the life of Hikaru Genji and his descendants (ten final chapters, dubbed as the "Uji

---

[14] J. M. Maki, op. cit., pp. 491-492.

[15] Even if it is impossible to speculate about Lady Murasaki's self-awareness as a writer in the same context as Umberto Eco did while introducing the notion of a model reader, parts of her diary in which she reflects the writing process of *The Tale of Genji*, as well as the parts of *The Tale of Genji* itself where she uses the character of Genji to explain her theory of the novel or writes about the specifics of the *monogatari* genre, seem to show she had at least some awareness of the relationship between the author, the novel and its readers (she mentions female readership of *monogatari* in the chapter *Hotaru – Fireflies* in Seidensticker translation referenced in this article). Cf. J. M. Maki, op. cit., pp. 492-493.

chapters,"[16] that take place after the death – or exit – of the main protagonist). Genji, also referred to as "the Shining Prince" is the son of Emperor, removed from the line of succession due to political reasons and the fact that his mother – the Emperor's most beloved consort (known to the readers of the novel as Lady Kiritsubo[17]) – was of low rank. The plot focuses mainly on Genji's romantic life, his numerous, often successful – after all, he is a "jewel beyond the compare"[18] – courtships, a few heartbreaks and the rivalry between himself and fellow aristocrats. Besides portraying the complicated relationships between the members of the nobility, the novel depicts in detail the culture and customs of the aristocratic society, and also conveys and preserves the philosophical and aesthetic values of the Heian period; among others, *mono no aware* (Jpn. 物の哀れ, literally "the pathos of things," also translated as "an empathy toward things"), *miyabi* (Jpn. 雅び, "elegance," "refinement" or "courtliness") and the Buddhist sense of impermanence.

In contrast with Lady Murasaki's monumental and detailed *opus magnum*, significantly less is known about her own life. With her personal name unknown (she is recognised by a pseudonym coined from the name of one of her characters and her father's court profession) and her own diary filled with "considerable gaps in what she is prepared to reveal,"[19] the authoress of *The Tale of Genji* is an enigmatic figure. Scholars agree about the key stages from her biography: being born to a family of the lower rank,[20] a remarkable – yet unconventional for a lady – education in Chinese classics that, as suggests Thomas Inge, might have brought her rather pity than joy,[21] a stay in Echizen Province, a short marriage that ended abruptly when her husband died during a cholera

---

[16] Despite the fact that the original manuscript no longer exists, it is known that the novel had been written chapter by chapter in instalments and the attribution of the final chapters to Murasaki Shikibu is questioned by some scholars. Cf. R. Tyler, *The Disaster of the Third Princess. Essays on* The Tale of Genji, p. 158.

[17] It is worth pointing here that in the original novel most of the characters were not given an explicit name, as it was not customary to casually use person's given name in the Heian period. Characters in the text were therefore referred with their rank, function or honorific (and sometimes – which could potentially be even more confusing, as it changed throughout the novel – their relation to other characters).

[18] M. Shikibu, *The Tale of Genji*, p. 48.

[19] R. Bowring, op. cit., p. 4.

[20] While it is established that she was a member of the Fujiwara clan, her branch of family was not in power, nor was it considered significant in the grand scheme of things.

[21] T. Inge, *Lady Murasaki and the Craft of Fiction*, p. 9.

epidemic, and finally – her time spend at the Imperial court serving Empress Shōshi. Still, there are still periods of Lady Murasaki's life that remind undiscovered (this may be one of the reasons why in Edo period texts her biography became idealised and the authoress herself became a role model for Edo women[22]). What is known, however, is the fact that she used her own biography as an inspiration for *The Tale of Genji*, which shows excellent knowledge of court life along with Lady Murasaki's ability to depict the issues of living away from the capital city or the struggle of low-ranked families with the outstanding psychological insight and realism for which the novel is often praised.[23] The origin of *The Tale of Genji* is unknown – while popular culture often presents the novel as a gift for Empress Shōshi,[24] scholars like Haruo Shirane or Richard Bowring argue that it was most likely the death of Lady Murasaki's husband – and the loneliness that followed – which prompted her most notable literary work.[25]

The novel opens with the birth of the title hero and subsequent death of his mother, Lady Kiritsubo, when the protagonist is three years old. From the very beginning of the story Lady Murasaki contributes to her portrayal of Prince Genji as the ideal man: even as a young child he is quickly recognised as a beauty beyond comparison and despite his mother's low rank Hikaru quickly becomes Emperor's favourite son ("the new child was [the Emperor's] private treasure, so to speak, upon whom to lavish uninhibited affection"[26]). Genji's childhood days at the court are careless and peaceful and during his coming-of-age ceremony he easily surpasses every other male with his good manners and chivalry, the graceful movements he exhibits while dancing and, of course, perfect knowledge of poetry, music and other "compulsory subjects."[27] All these traits, deeply rooted in Heian culture – compulsory, as stated by Lady Murasaki herself – reaffirm his depiction as the perfect man. By that time Genji is already a heart-throb

---

[22] Cf. S. Naito, *Beyond The Tale of Genji: Murasaki Shikibu as Icon and Exemplum in Seventeenth- and Eighteenth-Century Popular Japanese Texts for Women*, pp. 47-78.

[23] Cf. J. M. Maki, op. cit., p. 480.

[24] Cf. for example *Sennen no Koi – Hikaru Genji monogatari*, dir. Horikawa Tonkō, Japan 2001 or *Genji Monogatari: Sennen no Nazo*, dir. Yasuo Tsuruhasi, Japan 2011.

[25] H. Shirane, *Traditional Japanese Literature: An Anthology*, p. 293; R. Bowring, op. cit., p. 4.

[26] M. Shikibu, op. cit., p. 4.

[27] Ibidem, p. 14.

among the court ladies ("He was handsomer than the crown prince [...] well thought of by the whole court,"[28] "The lesser ladies crowded about, not in the least ashamed to show their faces, all eager to amuse him, though aware that he set them off to disadvantage"[29]), including Lady Fujitsubo, his stepmother (this forbidden love is the main theme of the first part of the novel), yet his first arranged marriage is an unhappy one. Both Genji and his wife, Lady Aoi, struggle to communicate and the young prince seeks extramarital happiness (which later ends with Aoi's tragic death), engaging in numerous yet unfulfilling love affairs. Throughout the novel Genji meets multiple ladies of various backgrounds – he courts each of them with proper attention, carefully chosen poems and gifts, which shows not only proper education of the protagonist, but also his selfless gallantry, adored by the ladies depicted in the novel... and those who read it as well. It is only after Genji meets young Murasaki that he falls in love and it is his relationship with Murasaki that drives the plot of the novel (the name of that particular heroin soon became a pseudonym of the authoress, which – as underlined by Maki following the thought of Ishimura Teikichi – itself points to the major popularity of the novel back in the Heian period[30]). Unlike her ideal prince, Murasaki is far from perfect; while kind and resembling the beauty of Lady Fujitsubo, Genji's beloved is yet a diamond in the rough. The difference in portraying these two protagonists is particularly interesting in the context of how the readers could have related to the novel's characters. While no real man could have possibly competed with an ideal hero (after all, "He had grown into a lad of such beauty that he hardly seemed meant for this world"[31]), court ladies reading Murasaki's story could have easily understood the struggles she encountered[32] and even see themselves in her.

---

[28] Ibidem, p. 16

[29] Ibidem, p. 13.

[30] As J. M. Maki states, "it seems entirely natural that the name of the principal female character of such a popular novel should have been given to the author as a sort of nickname". Cf. eadem, *Lady Murasaki and* The *Genji Monogatari*, p. 482.

[31] M. Shikibu, op. cit., p. 13.

[32] Royall Tyler presents a detailed study of Murasaki's complicated personality and the troubles she encounters throughout the novel in his article entitled *"I Am I": Genji and Murasaki*. Cf. R. Tyler, *"I Am I": Genji and Murasaki*, pp. 435–480.

2. POP-CULTURAL FRAMEWORK: GENJI IS LOVED

Like many novels appraised in modern times, *The Tale of Genji* soon gained a significant amount of readers and became popular among its targeted recipients. Especially those ladies of aristocracy who served at the court of Heian-kyō were able to access new scrolls easily as every chapter was distributed in many copies.[33] Obtaining the whole novel, a version consisting of all the chapters, was a real challenge. The daughter of Sugawara no Takasue, often referred to as "Lady Sarashina," mentioned such a struggle in her diary (*Sarashina nikki*, lit. "the Diary of Sarashina")[34] and was more than willing to read every part of *The Tale of Genji*. She openly writes:

> I read a few volumes of *Genji monogatari* and longed for the rest, but as I was still a stranger here [in the Capital, Heian-kyō – A.K. & J.M.-K] I had no way of finding them. I was all impatience and yearning, and in my mind was always praying that I might read all the books of *Genji monogatari* from the very first one.[35]

This emotional relationship with the text of the novel and its main protagonist allows us to look at Heian ladies from a different angle, using categories from modern popular culture. The first readers of *The Tale* bear a lot of similarities with quite modern fans of contemporary fictional characters. Again, that is not to say *The Tale of Genji* functions exactly as a work of 21st century popular culture – yet, some parallels regarding its reception are more than intriguing enough to be mentioned here.

We base our understanding of popular culture on the works of John Fiske, Dominic Strinati, John Storey and Marcel Danesi. Those scholars have distinguished between popular culture and mass culture and have based their definitions of a pop-culture product on the presence of particular characteristics: easiness of presenting and perceiving,

---

[33] On the distribution of *The Tale*, see for example I. Morris, *The World of the Shining Prince: Court Life in Ancient Japan*, pp. 263f.

[34] Similarly to the case of Murasaki Shikibu, her real name is unknown – in the classic Japanese literature she is known only by the name of her father. In her diary she also alludes to the name of the region "Sarashina", which resulted in her moniker "Lady Sarashina".

[35] *The Diary of Lady Sarashina (1009-1059)*, p. 18.

entertainment elements, fulfilling the needs of large audience, spreading the meanings and values, points of contact with the group which dominates in the society and grass-roots activity of the recipients and their participation in culture (active group of fans and large amount of culture texts, referring to the pop-culture product).[36] What is even more important to notice, in the light of their theories, a pop-culture product might emerge in any time and any place. Strinati explicitly writes that "popular culture can be found in different societies, within different groups in societies, and among societies and groups in different historical periods."[37] Likewise, Danesi opens his book entitled *Popular Culture: Introductory Perspectives* with a reference to Herodotus, who recorded various songs and performances during his travels, after all "history records that popular forms of entertainment have always existed."[38] That is why we feel justified to look at Genji as a hero and Lady Murasaki's novel as a whole through a pop-cultural prism.

A brief overview of what we already know about *The Tale of Genji*, its context and reception, proves that aforementioned similarities are easy to spot. Although a thousand years old, *The Tale* fulfils the criteria of a pop-cultural project in terms of its reception. Let us take a look at those particular characteristics. First of all, ease of presentation and perception – the novel was written in Japanese, and therefore it could have reached a larger reading public. While "it is highly improbable that Murasaki had male readers in mind while she was writing,"[39] using the Japanese language, in which both men and women of the Heian period were fluent,[40] made her novel easily accessible for any nobleman or woman and soon *The Tale of Genji* captured "a goodly number of readers among the men"[41] as well, including Emperor Ichijō himself[42] and prominent members of Fujiwara clan.[43] The method of notation is equally significant – Lady Murasaki used mainly *kana* syllabaries (*hiragana*,

---

[36]   Cf. J. Fiske, *Understanding Popular Culture*; D. Strinati, *An Introduction to Theories of Popular Culture*; J. Storey, *An Introduction to Cultural Theory and Popular Culture*; M. Danesi, *Popular Culture: Introductory Perspectives*.

[37]   D. Strinati, op. cit., p. xiv.

[38]   M. Danesi, op. cit., p. vii.

[39]   J. M. Maki, op. cit., p. 493.

[40]   R. Bowring, op. cit., p. 11.

[41]   J. M. Maki, op. cit., p. 493.

[42]   Ibidem.

[43]   S. Naito, *Beyond* The Tale of Genji: *Murasaki Shikibu as Icon and Exemplum in Seventeenth- and Eighteenth-Century Popular Japanese Texts for Women*, p. 48, footnote 2.

katakana), instead of the much more complicated *kanji* signs, under-stood by few recipients (it is worth mentioning that this way of writing proved to be challenging for modern translators). Scroll illustrations of the story quickly followed (as pointed by Akiko Hirota, it was customary for Heian period romances to be read aloud with pictures being shown in addition to the text[44]) making it even easier for court ladies to get fa-miliar with the Shining Prince and his story.

What is more, the genre of *monogatari* itself is, as already noted, one of the most popular genre of Heian literature, henceforth *The Tale of Genji* perfectly fits the needs of the readers and the spirit of the time. Following Heian customs – and the tastes of readers, shaped by the spir-it of aestheticism – Lady Murasaki also introduced hundreds of poems to her work, showing her erudition which relates to literary genre syn-cretism (e.g., usage of extra forms of storytelling) and the use of collage, often used in modern works of pop-culture.[45] Filling the novel with nu-merous poems also contributes to presenting Prince Genji as the most educated hero of all in addition to his flawless beauty and outstanding dancing skills. As already stated, "poetry was an intensely social activ-ity"[46] in the Heian period, serving not only as a usual form of commu-nication between aristocrats but also as a proof of required knowledge of classic Chinese works (thus poetry competitions were not unusual[47]) and attention to form (the latter was the most important element which organised the whole life of Heian court). The characters in *The Tale of Genji*, reflecting the life of real aristocrats, also speak in poems – and of course the ones composed by Prince Genji time and again prove to be exceptional, which only adds to his portrait as a culturally competent, therefore perfect, Heian courtier and male.

Secondly, entertaining elements are a key feature of every work of popular culture. They are also present in the understanding of *The Tale*. According to Minamoto Tamenori, governor of the province of Mikawa who lived at the turn of 10th and 11th century, "the novel is a work which pleases women."[48] His words seem to reflect general approach towards

---

[44] A. Hirota, The Tale of Genji: *From Heian Classic to Heisei Comic*, p. 29.
[45] On collage and bricolage, see: M. Danesi, op. cit., pp. 29ff.
[46] R. Bowring, op. cit., p. 5.
[47] Ibidem.
[48] He stated that in his work entitled *Sanbōe* or *Sambōe-kotoba* ("Illustrations of the Three Jewels", a collection of anecdotes, serving as an introduction to Buddhism). See: *Traditional Japanese Literature: An Anthology, Beginnings to 1600*, pp. 214ff.

monogatari in the Heian period – as Haruo points, *monogatari* were considered "a popular pastime among nobility"[49] rather than an intellectual challenge, both because of their content and because of the simplicity of their writing style (Japanese *kana*). *The Tale of Genji* was written by a woman for women and about women[50] – and the court ladies in Heiankyō were the first and the most enthusiastic readers of the novel. In her novel Lady Murasaki spoke the language of Heian court ladies – both literary, using the Japanese language, which, while understood by both genders, belonged to the women ("women had to recourse to Japanese and began to make it their own, creating a medium for the expression of their special concerns,"[51] points Bowring) and metaphorically, giving their readers the joy of reading about a perfect prince and a perfect love. Thus, their needs were fulfilled, which corresponds with another characteristic of a work of pop culture. Lady Murasaki created an ideal hero – shining (*nomen omen!*) example of all virtues and merits, desired in a perfect man of the Heian period. Handsome, educated, flawless and talented beyond imagination – Prince Genji won the attention and admiration not only of fictional heroines, but also of real court ladies. Portrayed far too idealistically (of which Lady Murasaki seems to be aware: "to recount all his virtues would, I fear, give rise to a suspicion that I distort the truth."[52]) Genji has become a perfect tool for fulfilling the needs of the readers: *The Tale of Genji* was meant for noble women and served as their entertainment.[53] This is also in accordance with both emotional nature of works of pop culture and their ability of celebrity making (here it is Prince Genji who – regardless of his fictional status – is treated almost like an existing celebrity by Heian court ladies) – two important features mentioned by Danesi.[54]

However, *The Tale of Genji* served not only as a source of entertainment, but also spread meaning and values significant to its audience. As already noted, Lady Murasaki's work consolidated most of values

---

49 H. Shirane, The Tale of Genji *and the Dynamics...*, p. 5.
50 This is exactly the phrase used by scholar Tamagami Takuya: *The Tale of Genji* was written "by a woman, for women, about [the world of] women". Quoted by Satoko Naito, op. cit., p. 48.
51 R. Bowring, op. cit., p. 12.
52 M. Shikibu, op. cit., p. 14.
53 Cf. L. Cook, *Genre Trouble: Medieval Commentaries and Canonization of* The Tale of Genji, p. 138.
54 M. Danesi, op. cit., pp. 104ff.

of the Heian period, such as *mono no aware* or *miyabi*. The clear and evident emphasis on values glorified by Heian aristocracy shows also the importance of noble people of the time – which is strongly relevant in this context, as the work of popular culture should also correspond with the life of a dominant social group. As we underlined before: the life of the Heian period in Japanese history concentrated on aristocracy alone. All noble gentlemen and ladies lived (or wished to live) in the capital city and considered the rest of the country barbaric. Therefore, only the aristocracy was responsible for creating the culture and only the aristocracy was its recipient. Furthermore, the nobility is to be thought of as the only culturally qualified subject.[55] This leads to an interesting paradox – while *The Tale of Genji* was in no way intended for "general circulation"[56] if talking about the Japanese society of the Heian period as a whole, in terms of court culture, the novel certainly reached almost all the members of the one society that – in their own view – mattered.[57]

The last characteristic of a work of pop culture is connected to the grass-roots activity of the recipients and their participation in culture. According to John Fiske, the pop-culture product should be an inspiration for creating the recipients' very own culture texts.[58] Court ladies, who adored Genji and could have identified with the love of his life, Murasaki, have been rewriting the story of the Shining Prince, supplementing it with their own additions and plots, or even changing some scenes and chapters. It is worth mentioning, especially in the light of pop-cultural studies, that such practices started very quickly and that while Lady Murasaki's original manuscript no longer exists, there are numerous copies (which differ between one another). This proves that *The Tale of Genji* – as any modern work of pop culture – had a deep impact on both culture and society, inspiring its readers to create their own texts which "adapted and translated *The Tale of Genji* into many genres and forms, thereby making it highly popular."[59] Surprising as it might

[55] This resonates with theory of John Fiske who proves that pop-culture fans must have culture competences. See J. Fiske, op. cit., p. 118.

[56] J. M. Maki, op. cit., s. 495.

[57] In rough estimation of Ivan Morris, the whole population of Heian Japan was about five million people, one percent of that number lived in the capital and only one tenth of this one percent – around 5,000 people – were a part of noble rank hierarchy. Cf. I. Morris, op. cit., p. 79.

[58] On the active participation of the people in the creation of popular culture, see for example J. Fiske, op. cit., pp. 25ff.

[59] H. Shirane, The Tale of Genji *and the Dynamics...*, p. 9.

be, the court ladies' modified versions of *The Tale of Genji* would be, on elementary comparison level, not that much different from the modern phenomenon of fan fiction.

Creating a complex web of references to *The Tale* started as early as in 11th century, when Heian court ladies wrote about the novel in their diaries – the diary of lady Sarashina among them, as well as the diary of Lady Murasaki herself. References to *The Tale of Genji* were present in the prose as well – one of the examples may be *Yowa no nezame* (also known as *Yoru no nezame*), another *tsukuri monogatari* written in the late 11th century. The exact date and the author remain unknown, and only part of the novel has survived to our times. Still, we know that *Yowa no nezame* tells the tragic story of a lady called Naka no Kimi, her older sister Ōigimi and Chunagon, the Middle Counselor.[60] The web of references, contexts and inspirations seems to prove how fast *The Tale* and its hero became an inseparable part of Japanese culture. That is why Haruo Shirane uses the term "Genji culture," explaining The Tale of Genji in *Envisioning:*

> The history of the reception of *The Tale of Genji* is no less than a cultural history of Japan, for the simple reason that the *Genji* has had a profound impact at various levels of culture in every historical period since its composition, including the 21st century, producing what is called a "Genji culture."[61]

Not only inspiring literary allusions, parodies, Noh theatre and other genres – *The Tale of Genji,* in periods following the Heian era, even became a source for Edo courtesans' names or incense contents.[62]

Back to the Heian period and the pop-cultural context, it is interesting that for some aristocratic ladies the boundaries between the real and the fictional seemed to blur. Namely, the Shining Prince was seen as a true male, ready to enter into court life (and the lives of his devoted readers). None other living man could even dream to reach the perfection of Prince Genji. The case of "fiction above reality" can be illustrated by the diaries of Lady Murasaki herself. She scarcely writes about everyday life – actually, Heian diaries were rarely composed

---

[60]   A short summary of the plot can be found in E. Miner, H. Odagiri, R. E. Morrell, *The Princeton Companion to Classical Japanese Literature*, pp. 259f.

[61]   H. Shirane, The Tale of Genji *and the Dynamics…*, p. 1.

[62]   Ibidem, p. 39.

as detailed journals, occupied with activities of mundane existence – and when she does, "her life in the court seems to have been none too pleasant."[63] Thus it is no wonder that even in her notes references to her hero and reflections on writing are more than numerous. The imaginary world of her work seemed to be more interesting than the real court life. One of the most well-known passages from Lady Murasaki's diary clearly alludes that:

> The First Officer of the Light Bodyguard said, "I think Lady Murasaki must be somewhere here!".
> I listened, thinking, "How can she be here in a place where there is no such graceful person as Prince Genji?"[64]

The boundaries between fiction and reality faded also for other ladies, bedazzled by the Shining Prince. Lady Sarashina, belonging to the second circle of readers (the first one would consist of Lady Murasaki's fellow ladies at court), stands as a perfect example. According to Sonja Arntzen and Itō Moriyuki, translators of *The Sarashina Diary*, this very work "gives a compelling account of the powerful effect of reading on one's perception of oneself and the world, a phenomenon found in all literary cultures."[65] Lady Sarashina is full of emotions while reading and writing about Genji and *The Tale* and she seems to enjoy particular characters above other. For example, she dreams to be as beautiful as lady Yūgao (one of Genji's lovers), yet she identifies herself mostly with lady Ukifune, who waits for her beloved away from the capital:

> The only thing that I could think of was the Shining Prince who would some day come to me, as noble and beautiful as in the romance. If he came only once a year I, being hidden in a mountain villa like Lady Ukifune, would be content. I could live as heart-dwindlingly as that lady, looking at flowers, or moonlit snowy landscape, occasionally receiving long-expected lovely letters from my Lord! I cherished such fancies and imagined that they might be realized.[66]

[63]   J. M. Maki, op. cit., p. 487.
[64]   *Diaries of Court Ladies of Old Japan*, p. 105.
[65]   *The Sarashina Diary: A Woman's Life in Eleventh-Century Japan*, p. 17.
[66]   *The Diary of Lady Sarashina (1009–1059)*, p. 20.

As noted by Haruo Shirane, those feelings evoked by Shining Prince and Sarashina's emotions can be treated as a model example of the reception of *The Tale* among its female readers (and, often, writers as well): "Writings on *Genji* by women, such as *Sarashina nikki* or *Mumyō-zōshi*, focus on the characters, with whom the authors closely identified, and read the *Genji* as a tale, for its story line and for exploring and understanding their own lives."[67] This, once again, shows two remarkable skills Murasaki possessed as a writer: descriptive realism, which allowed her to depict characters that belonged to the same world as her readers ("The characters move in an environment that was rightfully theirs because they were a part of the Imperial Court"[68]) and the ability to create a hero desired by all. The Shining Prince, the perfect male who outshined any real Heian courtier, along with detailed descriptions of his romances functions as a sort of projection for court ladies from the era. One might even say that reading *The Tale* would be a compensation of their unfulfilled dreams and desires – or simply a remedy for constant boredom, an everyday companion of aristocratic women confined behind blinds. The story of Prince Genji is not only a form of entertainment or a model of court life for those staying away from the capital – it is also a story of an ideal: a perfect male, his various lovers and a romantic love, rarely witnessed in the times of arranged political marriages.

Lastly, it would be worth noticing that while analysing *The Tale of Genji* as a popular culture product, one might at the same time notice a significant amount of parallelisms with the modern chick-lit novel (written for pure entertainment, by a woman for women) and their perception in society. Essential similarities are, among other things, a central protagonist and plot revolving around him (the plot of the novel is character-oriented rather than story-driven), carefully outlined minor characters (especially potential rivals who nevertheless do not match the hero as they lack in physical attractiveness and intellectual value; this literary method corresponds well with the concept of idealising the hero of the novel), an appropriate chosen one for the protagonist (unlike him, not ideal, and so female readers may identify with her) and emphasis on ludicity and entertainment (the novel should be easy to digest and read with pleasure, influence the culture and inspire

[67]   H. Shirane, The Tale of Genji *and the Dynamic...*, p. 20.
[68]   J. M. Maki, op. cit., p. 498.

fan fiction).[69] In the context of our paper, the first similarity seems to be particularly striking: Genji's importance and perfection, easily visible both in the content and in the structure of *The Tale*. "The shining Genji was dead, and there was no one quite like him,"[70] the authoress writes in the opening line of chapter 42, the first that deals with the absence of the hero. "No longer does one great figure dominate the story,"[71] points out Maki – along with Genji being gone the setting (moved from the capital to Uji area[72]) and the mood of the novel changed profoundly as well. Shifting the tone of the novel, Lady Murasaki shows that there was no other character – no other person – who could replace Genji and that his absence affected the very universe she created, not just the characters within it.

CONCLUSIONS

The Tale of Genji remains an exceptional work of literature in many aspects. Despite being first and foremost a historical classic, "now perceived, both in Japan and abroad, as one the most potent emblems of the imagined community of Japanese nation; as a masterpiece of Japanese literature, for which, and to which, Japan, its language, and its citizen are somehow responsible,"[73] it also proves to be relevant material when discussing topics usually connected with contemporary culture and society, like gender studies, modern literature theories[74] and cultural production analysis.

Exploring *The Tale* in the light of theories of popular culture once again shows the timelessness of Lady Murasaki's *opus magnum* and also leads to a better understanding of the relationship between the readers and the novel's eponymous protagonist. Although *The Tale of*

---

[69]   The authors of this paper have traced a surprising amount of similarities between Prince Genji and two modern heroes: Edward Cullen from *Twilight* series and Christian Grey from *Fifty Shades of Grey trilogy*. See: A. Kuchta, J. Malita, *50 twarzy Genjiego*, pp. 38–43.

[70]   M. Shikibu, op. cit., p. 735.

[71]   J. M. Maki, op. cit., p. 498.

[72]   While now a part of Kyōto city, back in the Heian period Uji was considered rather a rural area.

[73]   M. Emmerich, op. cit., p. 3.

[74]   Cf. B. Phillips, The Tale of Genji *as a Modern Novel*, pp. 373–390.

Genji is not exactly a product of what we now understand as pop-culture, it bears many similarities with modern works and the readers of the novel, court society of the Heian period, prove not to be entirely dissimilar from contemporary recipients of popular culture. The main character, Prince Hikaru Genji, an ideal male of Heian era, was adored by his fictional lovers and real-life readers alike. He transgressed the boundaries of a fictional tale, becoming a perfect – yet fantasy – male for ladies of the Heian aristocracy. As such, he does not differ that much from modern characters of popular culture, worshipped by fans. Lady Murasaki's creation of Prince Genji shows her knowledge of the readers' needs and understanding of their desires – she depicts a hero who encompasses all the desired personal traits and skills, who is handsome and dashing and easily suits the tastes of Heian court ladies. It was the character of Genji – not the plot – that drove the readers towards the novel and fuelled their imagination, reflected in their own texts. Therefore the Shining Prince made an impact not only on the fictional world he was a part of, but also left his elegant footprints on Japanese literature, culture and society.

BIBLIOGRAPHY

Bowring R., *The Cultural Background* [in:] *Murasaki Shikibu*, The Tale of Genji, R. Bowring (ed.), Cambridge UP, Cambridge 2004, pp. 1-21.

Cook L., *Genre Trouble: Medieval Commentaries and Canonization of* The Tale of Genji [in:] *Envisioning the Tale of Genji*, H. Shirane (ed.), Columbia University Press, New York 2008, pp. 129-153.

Danesi M., *Popular Culture: Introductory Perspectives*, Rowman & Littlefield, Lanham, MD 2012.

Emmerich M., The Tale of Genji: *Translation, Canonization, and World Literature*, Columbia University Press, New York 2013.

Envisioning the Tale of Genji: Media, Gender, and Cultural Production, H. Shirane (ed.), Columbia University Press, New York 2008.

Fiske J., *Understanding Popular Culture*, Routledge, London 2010.

Garfias R., *Music of a Thousand Autumns: The Tōgaku Style of Japanese Court Music*, University of California Press, Berkeley-Los Angeles 1975.

Hirota A., The Tale of Genji: *From Heian Classic to Heisei Comic*, "The Journal of Popular Culture", Vol. 31, Issue 2, Fall 1997, pp. 29-68.

Inge T., *Lady Murasaki and the Craft of Fiction*, "South Atlantic Review", Vol. 55, No. 2, May 1990, pp. 7-14.

Kuchta A., Malita J., *50 twarzy Genjiego*, "Torii. Magazyn totalnie o Japonii", No. 18, 2013, pp. 38-43.

Kuchta A., Malita J., „*Opowieść o Księciu Promienistym*": *fascynacja na granicy fikcji i rzeczywistości* [in:] *Literatura na granicach*, M. Błaszkowska et al. (eds.), AT Group, Kraków 2015, pp. 59-70.

Maki J. M., *Lady Murasaki and the* Genji Monogatari, "Monumenta Nipponica", Vol. 3, No. 2, July 1940, pp. 480-503.

Miner E., Odagiri H., Morrell R. E., *The Princeton Companion to Classical Japanese Literature*, Princeton University Press, Princeton 1988.

Morris I., *The World of the Shining Prince: Court Life in Ancient Japan*, Penguin Publishing Group, New York 1985.

Naito S., *Beyond* The Tale of Genji: *Murasaki Shikibu as Icon and Exemplum in Seventeenth- and Eighteenth-Century Popular Japanese Texts for Women*, "Early Modern Women: An Interdisciplinary Journal", Vol. 9, No. 1, Fall 2014, pp. 47-78.

Phillips B., The Tale of Genji *as a Modern Novel*, "The Hudson Review", Vol 63, No. 3, Autumn 2010, pp. 373-390.

Sarashina, *The Diary of Lady Sarashina (1009-1059)* [in:] *Diaries of Court Ladies of Old Japan*, A. Shepley Omori, K. Doi (trans. and ed.), Houghton Mifflin Company, Boston-New York 1920, pp. 3-68.

Shikibu M., *The Diary of Murasaki Shikibu* [in:] *Diaries of Court Ladies of Old Japan*, A. Shepley Omori, K. Doi (trans. and ed.), Houghton Mifflin Company, Boston-New York 1920, pp. 69-145.

Shikibu M., *The Tale of Genji*, E. G. Seidensticker (trans. and ed.), Charles E. Tuttle, Tokyo 1978.

Shirane H., The Tale of Genji *and the Dynamic of Cultural Production: Canonization and Popularization* [in:] *Envisioning the Tale of Genji*, H. Shirane (ed.), Columbia University Press, New York 2008, pp. 1-47.

Shirane H., *Traditional Japanese Literature: An Anthology, Beginnings to 1600*, Columbia University Press, New York 2008.

Storey J., *An Introduction to Cultural Theory and Popular Culture. Eight edition*, Routledge, London-New York 2017.

Strinati D., *An Introduction to Theories of Popular Culture*, Routledge, London-New York 2004.

The Sarashina Diary: A Woman's Life in Eleventh-Century Japan, S. Arntzen, I. Moriyuki (trans. and ed.), Columbia University Press, New York 2014.

Traditional Japanese Literature: An Anthology, Beginnings to 1600, H. Shirane (ed.), Columbia University Press, New York 2008.

Tyler R., *"I Am I": Genji and Murasaki*, "Monumenta Nipponica", Vol. 54, No. 4, Winter 1999, pp. 435-480.

Tyler R., *The Disaster of the Third Princess. Essays on* The Tale of Genji, ANU E Press, Canberra 2009.

INTERNET SOURCES USED

[www 01] https://terebess.hu/english/kawabata.html (accessed: 28.07.2019)

Sennen no koi – Hikaru Genji monogatari (千年の恋.ひかる源氏物語), dir. Horikawa Tonkō, Japan 2001.

Genji Monogatari: Sennen no Nazo (源氏物語.千年の謎), dir. Yasuo Tsuruhasi, Japan 2011.

KATARZYNA BORKOWSKA
ⓘ https://orcid.org/0000-0002-3963-1569

CICERO AND MALE VIRTUE

Abstract: In the final years of the Republic, with the inclusion of new nations under Roman rule, there was a growing need to define Roman identity. This identity was constructed around the concept of male virtue (*virtus*) and stood in opposition to foreign influences. Consequently, some aspects of culture came to be seen as threatening to the ideal of Roman masculinity. Cicero is known to have been criticised for overly engaging in Greek education and to have featured feminine qualities in his oratory conduct. Aware of the gravity of these accusations, Cicero made much effort to recreate Roman ideals and male virtue in such a way, as to match the qualities he had been criticized for. Referring to selected passages from Cicero's work I aim to describe his attempts to reinvent the concept of *virtus* in order to present himself and his literary interests within the category of masculinity.

Keywords: Cicero, virtue, masculinity

As we learn from Plutarch and Quintilian, and can deduce from his own texts, Cicero was criticised for his literary interests and education in Greek philosophy, as well as for his style and performance as an orator, too feminine for the Roman taste. In order to examine the reasons behind the accusations that Cicero had to face, I shall briefly discuss the opinions expressed by Cato the Censor (as referred by Plutarch) and Julius Caesar, presenting the attitudes towards cultural practices (especially foreign) within Roman society of the Late Republic. Following Brian Krostenko's steps, I take Roman virtue (*virtus*) to be constructed in opposition to individualism and aestheticism. Both these qualities were perceived as Greek and feminine, and both were closely associated with culture, whence the apparent superstition against culture that it weakens male virtue arose. An analysis of Cicero's texts reveals that, aware of the said superstition, he tried to defend the study of literature and philosophy by grounding it in the socially valuable, masculine sphere. He emphasises the benefits poetry can bring to the community in *Pro Archia*; in *Tusculan Disputations* he redefines *virtus*, stressing its relation to masculinity, but emphasising one component – a strength of character that only a study of philosophy can shape. In *De Officiis* he advocates moderation between feminine and masculine qualities; in *De Oratore* he argues for the value of humour and claims that it is a proper and elegant tool to complement traditional Roman dignity. He does not wish to play a revolutionary role. Even as he advocates for the qualities that were seen as threatening to traditional Roman values, he does so from the position of a guardian and continuator of these values. What he proposes, is a new, cultural interpretation of the way of the elders (*mos maiorum*) and the reinvention of the ideal of the proper Roman citizen (*vir bonus*) as an educated gentleman.

The incident of Cato the Elder expelling the Greek philosophers – Carneades the Skeptic and Diogenes the Stoic – from Rome in 155 BC became a symbol of his aversion to Greek philosophy and Greek culture.[1] Plutarch reports that from the very beginning when the fame of the philosophers (and Carneades in particular) began to spread, Cato suspected that it may have a negative influence on the value system of young Romans.

> (…) Cato, from the very moment when the enthusiasm about these theories began to overflow the city, feared for the youth not to turn their ambitions to admiring a reputation based on mere words rather than achievements on the battlefield. When the fame of the philosophers kept advancing in the city and their first speeches were interpreted in front of the Senate (…), by a pretext, he determined to expel the philosophers from the city altogether and he came forward to speak to the Senate: (…) "we need to decide as quickly as possible what should be done about this embassy, so that these men can return to practicing dialectics with the Greek children in their schools, while the Roman youth shall obey their rulers and laws, as they did before." This he did not do – as some seem to believe – because he despised Carneades, but rather striking against philosophy in general and by his ambition criticising all Greek culture and education (πᾶσαν Ἑλληνικὴν μοῦσαν καὶ παιδείαν).[2]

---

[1]   As referred by Plutarch – Plut., *Cat. Ma.*, 22.1-23.3.
[2]   ὁ δὲ Κάτων ἐξ ἀρχῆς τε τοῦ ζήλου τῶν λόγων παραρρέοντος εἰς τὴν πόλιν ἤχθετο φοβούμενος, μὴ τὸ φιλότιμον ἐνταῦθα τρέψαντες οἱ νέοι τὴν ἐπὶ τῷ λέγειν δόξαν

Cato thought the influence of Greek philosophy could be threatening to Roman virtue (*virtus*), which was built on respect for tradition and law. He was known to have spoken against Socrates, because "he became violent in his chattery and attempted, however he could, to tyrannise his homeland, abolishing the customs and inciting opinions contrary to the law in his fellow citizens."[3] As written by Quintilian, Carneades spoke equally confidently against justice, as he did for it.[4] Cato presented the speech against justice as a direct attack on *virtus* and so he banished the philosophers, for many becoming a true representation of the virtue he defended. Erich S. Gruen argues with Plutarch, claiming that Cato did not have contempt for philosophy and Greek culture in general. He just required it not to overstep its proper place, as Carneades did, by gaining such popularity among the Roman youth.[5]

> Over refined philosophic study leads to self-absorption and empty
> phrase-mongering that distract one from more productive pursuits, name-
> ly, commitment to established norms, institutions, and traditions. His
> purpose was not to deliver wholesale censure of philosophy but to set up

ἀγαπήσωσι μᾶλλον τῆς ἀπὸ τῶν ἔργων καὶ τῶν στρατειῶν. ἐπεὶ δὲ προῦβαινεν ἡ δόξα τῶν φιλοσόφων ἐν τῇ πόλει καὶ τοὺς πρώτους λόγους αὐτῶν πρὸς τὴν σύγκλητον ἀνὴρ ἐπιφανὴς σπουδάσας αὐτὸς καὶ δεηθεὶς ἡρμήνευσε, Γάϊος Ἀκίλιος, ἔγνω μετ᾽ εὐπρεπείας ἀποδιοπομπήσασθαι τοὺς φιλοσόφους ἅπαντας ἐκ τῆς πόλεως, καὶ παρελθὼν εἰς τὴν σύγκλητον ἐμέμψατο τοῖς ἄρχουσιν, ὅτι πρεσβεία κάθηται πολὺν χρόνον ἄπρακτος ἀνδρῶν, οἳ περὶ παντὸς οὗ βούλοιντο ῥᾳδίως πείθειν δύνανται· δεῖν οὖν τὴν ταχίστην γνῶναί τι καὶ ψηφίσασθαι περὶ τῆς πρεσβείας, ὅπως οὗτοι μὲν ἐπὶ τὰς σχολὰς τραπόμενοι διαλέγωνται παισὶν Ἑλλήνων, οἱ δὲ Ῥωμαίων νέοι τῶν νόμων καὶ τῶν ἀρχόντων ὡς πρότερον ἀκούωσι. ταῦτα δ᾽ οὐχ, ὡς ἔνιοι νομίζουσι, Καρνεάδη δυσχεράνας ἔπραξεν, ἀλλ᾽ ὅλως φιλοσοφίᾳ προσκεκρουκὼς καὶ πᾶσαν Ἑλληνικὴν μοῦσαν καὶ παιδείαν ὑπὸ φιλοτιμίας προπηλακίζων. – Plut., *Cat.*, 22.4–23.1.

3 καὶ Σωκράτη φησὶ λάλον καὶ βίαιον γενόμενον ἐπιχειρεῖν τρόπῳ δυνατὸς ἦν, τυραννεῖν τῆς πατρίδος, καταλύοντα τὰ ἔθη καὶ πρὸς ἐναντίας τοῖς νόμοις δόξας ἕλκοντα καὶ μεθιστάντα τοὺς πολίτας. – Plut., *Cat.*, 23.1.

4 "nec Carneades ille, qui Romae audiente Censorio Catone non minoribus viribus contra iustitiam dicitur disseruisse quam pridie pro iustitia dixerat, iniustus ipse vir fuit." – Quint., *Inst.*, 12.1.35.

5 Thomas Habinek presents a similar opinion – he emphasises that foreign literature and culture is good for the Roman state as long as it is under control. Vide T. N. Habinek, *The Politics of Roman Empire: Writing, Identity and Empire in Ancient Rome*.

that discipline as a foil in order to better express the distinctiveness of Roman values.[6]

Cato's critique of Socrates can be interpreted similarly: "The criticism of Socrates contains an interesting implication. Cato did not fault the famous Athenian on grounds of perniciousness of philosophy. Rather, he censured Socrates for despotic ambitions that, if fulfilled, would undermine institutions and traditions."[7] From the point of view presented by Gruen we can arrive at a conclusion that shall become relevant later in this paper, that the *virtus* guarded by Cato was focused on the public sphere (traditions and institutions). Socrates' quest for the truth of the human soul introduced a form of individualism dangerous to Roman values. What also focuses my attention in the quoted passage of Plutarch, is his reference to "all of Greek culture and education" (πᾶσαν Ἑλληνικὴν μοῦσαν καὶ παιδείαν) – and it is because of its resemblance to the piece of text that I will discuss next. Particularly the resemblance of the language, although it is not the same language.

In the very beginning of the *Commentaries on the Gallic War,* Julius Caesar distinguished the Belgae among other Gallic peoples on the account of their bravery (*fortitudo*):

> All Gaul is divided into three parts, one of which inhabit the Belgae, another the Aquitani, the third one those, in their language, Celts, in ours called Gauls. These all differ among themselves in language, institutions and laws. (…) The bravest (*fortissimi*) of them all are the Belgae, because they are the furthest away from the culture and education (*cultu atque humanitate*) of (our) province, and the merchants, who usually bring those things that tend to effeminate the mind (*ad effeminandos animos pertinent*), reach them the least often; they are also the closest to the Germans, who live beyond the Rhine, and with whom they are continuously at war.[8]

---

[6]   E. S. Gruen, *Culture and National Identity in the Republican Rome*, p. 67.

[7]   Ibidem, p. 65.

[8]   "Gallia est omnis divisa in partes tres, quarum unam incolunt Belgae, aliam Aquitani, tertiam qui ipsorum lingua Celtae, nostra Galli appellantur. Hi omnes lingua, institutis, legibus inter se differunt. (…) Horum omnium fortissimi sunt Belgae, propterea quod a cultu atque humanitate provinciae longissime absunt, minimeque ad eos mercatores saepe commeant atque ea quae ad effeminandos animos pertinent important, proximique sunt Germanis, qui trans Rhenum incolunt, quibuscum continenter bellum gerunt." – Caes., *Gal.*, 1.1.

The reason for the Belgae's exceptional courage is apparently so obvious that it does not require much argumentation; it is actually the first observation about Gallic societies that Caesar makes in the book. They are located the furthest away from the more civilised territories and therefore do not experience the feminising influence of culture and luxury. Apart from that, they get to practice their military skills regularly, due to the constant war over their territory. Caesar names the absence of *cultus* and *humanitas* as the first cause for the Belgae's *fortitudo*. Second come the things that effeminate souls brought by the merchants, but who usually do not reach them. It is fair to assume that these would include decorative items, such as sophisticated fabrics and jewellery, cosmetic products: oils, balms, perfumes, and simple works of art, like painted pottery. All falling under the category of culture. Military practice is listed as the third. There may be doubts as to whether this is a positive description of the Belgae. Some might argue that they are presented as savages – with no culture or education. *Fortitudo*, however, is not a word someone would use to express their contempt. In fact, Cicero in his *Tusculan Disputations* claims that *fortitudo* is the main and most important aspect of virtue.

> Although we call all the proper states of mind virtues (*virtutes*), it is not a proper name for them all, but after this one that excels all the others, all are named. For virtue (*virtus*) is called after man (*vir*); the quality most proper to a man is valour (*fortitudo*), that has two most important functions: contempt of death and miseries, and we must use them if we wish to obtain virtue, or rather if we wish to be men, because virtue's name derives from men (*viris*).[9]

Virtus is the most excellent quality of a man, and from man it takes its name (*appellata est enim ex viro virtus*). The link between courage and masculinity is straightforward, and – according to Cicero's explanation of *virtus* – masculinity is good by definition. However unsure we may be about Caesar's attitude towards the Belgae, we can clearly see that he

---

[9] "cum omnes rectae animi adfectiones virtutes appellentur, non sit hoc proprium nomen omnium, sed ab ea quae una ceteris excellebat omnes nominatae sint. appellata est enim ex viro virtus; viri autem propria maxime est fortitudo, cuius munera duo sunt maxima: mortis dolorisque contemptio. utendum est igitur his, si virtutis compotes vel potius si viri volumus esse, quoniam a viris virtus nomen est mutuata." – Cic., *Tusc.*, 2.43.

makes an immediate connection between a certain discipline of mind – presented as masculine – and the abstinence from culture and education. The Belgae are just an example, an anecdotal evidence of such a process taking place – culture and education feminising male minds. The words Caesar uses, *cultus* and *humanitas*, resemble Plutarch's μοῦσα and παιδεία. It does not seem improbable that both authors referred to the same concept, one that was also advocated by Cato and well known to the Roman public.

Let us take a closer look at what it meant to a Roman of the Late Republic – to become feminine. Cicero had given this topic some thought, himself being criticised for insufficient masculinity. He by no means restrained himself from the influence of *cultus* and *humanitas*. He was a sophisticated man, who cherished his education in Greek literature and philosophy and could appreciate a beautiful work of art. Because of such inclinations, both his masculinity and his patriotism were questioned. Plutarch reports him to be called by his peers "a Greek and a scholar" (Γραικὸς καὶ σχολαστικός),[10] Quintilian summarises his oratory practice as "softer than befits a man" (*viro molliorem*).[11] The accusations can be deduced in more details from the way Cicero confronts them in his work. One of the most interesting examples of Cicero reclaiming his name is his speech in defence of Archias, the Greek poet. The speech contains well known passages describing the benefits of literary studies, that are often referred to as a praise[12] or an encomium[13] of poetry. I am suggesting that it might be more appropriate to perceive these passages as an apology of poetry instead. Cicero himself underlines the unusual character of his performance – this is a speech that

[10] "καὶ τόν γε πρῶτον ἐν Ῥώμῃ χρόνον εὐλαβῶς διῆγε καὶ ταῖς ἀρχαῖς ὀκνηρῶς προσῄει καὶ παρημελεῖτο, ταῦτα δὴ τὰ Ῥωμαίων τοῖς βαναυσοτάτοις πρόχειρα καὶ συνήθη ῥήματα, Γραικὸς καὶ σχολαστικὸς ἀκούων." – Plut. *Cic.*, 5.

[11] "at M. Tullium non illum habemus Euphranorem circa plures artium species praestantem, sed in omnibus, quae in quoque laudantur, eminentissimum. quem tamen et suorum homines temporum incessere audebant ut tumidiorem et Asianum et redundantem et in repetitionibus nimium et in salibus aliquando frigidum et in compositione fractum, exultantem ac paene, quod procul absit, viro molliorem;" – Quint., *Inst.*, 12.10.12.

[12] E.g. "In the *Pro Archia*, it is Cicero's intention to play down the absence of evidential documents by a solemn praise of poetry" – M. von Albrecht, *Cicero's style*, 83.

[13] E.g. "It is the encomium of literature, however, for which *Pro Archia* is read and remembered." – D. H. Berry, *Literature and Persuasion in Cicero's Pro Archia*, p. 292; cf. "(…) in defence of (…) the Greek poet Archias (…) Cicero delivered a famous panegyric of the humanities." – P. McKendrick, *The Philosophical Books of Cicero*, p. 2.

goes against the customs of the court and of public speaking in general (*genere dicendi quod non modo a consuetudine iudiciorum verum etiam a forensi sermone abhorreat*).[14] He does not focus on Archias as an individual – his particular case could be concluded in one paragraph; rather, Cicero stresses the defendant's value as a poet and the general value of poetry to society. More than a half of the whole text is devoted to that goal – proving that literary practice is worthy of a Roman citizen. The crafting of this speech was determined by public opinion. The connection between culture and femininity expressed by Julius Caesar in his *Commentaries on the Gallic War* resonated within Roman society. Had Cicero's crowd believed poetry socially valuable, the orator would not have had to go to such lengths to present it as such. He humbly asks his public to "endure the slightly looser manner of speaking about studies of culture and literature" (*patiamini de studiis humanitatis ac litterarum paulo loqui liberius*).[15]

As Brian Krostenko noticed, there are two crucial components based on which the Romans generally determined what was socially valuable: communalism and inaestheticism. These qualities were consequently seen as both masculine and Roman.[16] The Greek poet Archias represents the opposite categories of individualism and aestheticism. Accordingly, in order to prove Archias worthy, Cicero stresses the benefits that literature can bring to the public. He uses his own political career as an example, emphasising the importance of literary education in his service to the state. After referring to Archias' and his own – vulnerable to critique – engagement in literature, he makes sure to present the negative cases of more frivolous (more feminine in nature indeed, because focused on the individual, the aesthetic and the pleasant) cultural practices.

---

[14] "sed ne cui vestrum mirum esse videatur, me in quaestione legitima et in iudicio publico, cum res agatur apud praetorem populi Romani, lectissimum virum, et apud severissimos iudices, tanto conventu hominum ac frequentia hoc uti genere dicendi quod non modo a consuetudine iudiciorum verum etiam a forensi sermone abhorreat, quaeso a vobis ut in hac causa mihi detis hanc veniam accommodatam huic reo, vobis, quem ad modum spero, non molestam, ut me pro summo poeta atque eruditissimo homine dicentem hoc concursu hominum litteratissimorum, hac vestra humanitate, hoc denique praetore exercente iudicium, patiamini de studiis humanitatis ac litterarum paulo loqui liberius, et in eius modi persona quae propter otium ac studium minime in iudiciis periculisque tractata est uti prope novo quodam et inusitato genere dicendi." – Cic., *Arch.*, 3.

[15] Ibidem.

[16] B. Krostenko, *Cicero, Catullus and the Language of Social Performance*, pp. 31-32, 77-97.

Let the others be ashamed, if they devote their time to literature in such a way that nothing comes out of it, that it brings no use to the community, nor it is brought out in the public light; me on the other hand, why should I be ashamed, when all these years I have lived this way, judges, that no opportunity or convenience would ever draw me away from anything nor would leisure or pleasure distract me, nor would even sleep slow me down. In the end, why would anyone judge me, or thought it just to resent me, if, how much of other people's time is spent going around their own businesses, how much celebrating at the festivals on the holidays, how much on other pleasures and comforts for their souls and bodies, how much others contribute to early-day banquets, how much lastly to a game of chess or ball, that much I myself will devote to practice of these studies over and over again.[17]

He names those who devote themselves to literature without producing anything useful to the community (*nihil possint ex eis neque ad communem adferre fructum*), and then those who spend their time on festivals, games, banquets and other idle pleasures of body and mind. These examples serve to emphasise Cicero's practical and political approach to literature, as well as the diligence of his work.[18] They clearly demonstrate that he doesn't care for the recreational aspects of culture. Through the defence of Archias and the apology of poetry, aware of the

[17] "ceteros pudeat, si qui ita se litteris abdiderunt ut nihil possint ex eis neque ad communem adferre fructum neque in aspectum lucemque proferre; me autem quid pudeat qui tot annos ita vivo, iudices, ut a nullius umquam me tempore aut commodo aut otium meum abstraxerit aut voluptas avocarit aut denique somnus retardarit? qua re quis tandem me reprehendat, aut quis mihi iure suscenseat, si, quantum ceteris ad suas res obeundas, quantum ad festos dies ludorum celebrandos, quantum ad alias voluptates et ad ipsam requiem animi et corporis conceditur temporum, quantum alii tribuunt tempestivis conviviis, quantum denique alveolo, quantum pilae, tantum mihi egomet ad haec studia recolenda sumpsero – Cic., *Arch.*, 12-13.

[18] Later in his life he loses the argument of making a political use of his literary interests when he gets pushed away from his public function and stays in his villa in Tusculum. Then, he finds a new reason for his studies – he is going to create a new tradition of Roman philosophy, a proper Latin vocabulary, and in this way – conquer the last, so far undefeated Greek bastion. Nevertheless, he emphasises that he only took this task upon after having been released from his duties. "Cum defensionum laboribus senatoriisque muneribus aut omnino aut magna ex parte essem aliquando liberatus, rettuli me, Brute, te hortante maxime ad ea studia, quae retenta animo, remissa temporibus, longo intervallo intermissa revocavi, et cum omnium artium, quae ad rectam vivendi viam pertinerent, ratio et disciplina studio sapientiae, quae philosophia dicitur, contineretur, hoc mihi Latinis litteris inlustrandum putavi." – Cic., *Tusc.*, 1.1.

connotations, Cicero upholds himself. He makes every effort to place his literary interests in "a space made valuable by the actuating gaze of a Roman – because once there that aestheticism can serve useful function."[19] Poetry can and should be used for common good. It can serve political purposes. Its aesthetic values and its role in personal development (when it is not to serve the Republic) are mentioned shortly, close to the end of the apology, just before Cicero invokes the tradition of honouring poets. "Even if the great use of these studies were not apparent and if they were only aimed for pleasure, still, I believe, you would consider it the most cultural and noble (*humanissimam ac liberalissimam*)[20] form of recreation." For, he explains, it is the only one that fits every time, every age and every place.[21] The fragment praises literature as the most proper entertainment, an elegant way to enjoy oneself on every occasion. It is a not a genuine praise, because Cicero had said earlier that the recreational use of literature is shameful. But so are all other forms of entertainment, and more so than literature. The conditional sentence in the beginning of this fragment emphasises that the practical function of literary studies is indeed apparent and enjoyment of it is but a nice addition that should not be dwelled on.

While apologising for his – feminine in perception – qualities, Cicero does not go as far as to contradict Caesar's statement about the feminising power of culture; nor does he try to present feminine as positive. Rather, he describes a spectrum between masculinity and femininity. What is to be pursued is the harmony between the two – a harmony, but not equality. Cicero expresses this position in *De Officiis*:

> The way of standing, walking, seating, reclining, the expression of face and eyes and the gestures – all this should be kept in propriety (*decorum*).

---

[19] B. Krostenko, op. cit., p. 159.

[20] It is worth to notice that Cicero uses the word *humanissima* here. When the value of culture (*humanitas*) itself is at question, the adjective "cultural" (*humanum*) could be controversial. Perhaps it might also serve a role of recreating the meaning of *humanum* – together with *liberalis*, it stands for "worthy of a proper citizen". Of course *humanum* has many meanings, and the principal one is "human" or "of a man."

[21] "quod si non hic tantus fructus ostenderetur, et si ex his studiis delectatio sola peteretur, tamen, ut opinor, hanc animi remissionem humanissimam ac liberalissimam iudicaretis. nam ceterae neque temporum sunt neque aetatum omnium neque locorum; at haec studia adulescentiam acuunt, senectutem oblectant, secundas res ornant, adversis perfugium ac solacium praebent, delectant domi, non impediunt foris, pernoctant nobiscum, peregrinantur, rusticantur." – Cic. *Arch.*, 16.

In those things these two are to be most avoided, not to get feminine or soft (*effeminatum aut molle*) and not to get rough or rustic (*durum aut rusticum*). (…) Certain kinds of modesty are to be kept, especially having nature itself as a teacher and leader. There are two kinds of beauty: loveliness (*venustas*) and dignity (*dignitas*); loveliness we shall consider feminine, dignity – masculine. Therefore we shall remove from the male form all the undignified ornament and guard against similar faults in gesture and movements. For the way men in palestra move is often horrid, while many of the actors' gestures are not without silliness, and in both kinds simple and unaffected manner should be praised. (…) Further, we should apply neatness, not vexatious and sophisticated beyond measure, but peasantry and uncivilised (*inhumanam*) negligence should be just as much avoided. Similar reason should be applied to clothing, in which, just like in many other things, moderation is optimal (*mediocritas optima est*).[22]

It should be noted that he does not call the masculine extreme by its name, like he does with the feminine. It seems quite understandable, given all the positive connotations to the word *vir*, that Cicero himself discusses in the above-mentioned passage of *Tusculan Disputations* (2.43). Masculinity, traditionally viewed as ideal, cannot serve as the negative extreme. It seems that the end described as "rough or rustic" (*durum aut rusticum*) – both these words in Latin can mean uneducated, uncultivated – is something further away from the center, while masculinity lays somewhere between the rough end and the coveted harmony. A couple of sentences later, the opposition of the feminine and the masculine appears on seemingly more equal terms. Cicero proposes a medium between *venustas* and *dignitas* as optimal. It should not be overlooked that the said medium is not exactly halfway between the two. *Dignitas*

[22] "status incessus, sessio accubitio, vultus oculi manuum motus teneat illud decorum. Quibus in rebus duo maxime sunt fugienda, ne quid effeminatum aut molle et ne quid durum aut rusticum sit. (…) Retinenda igitur est huius generis verecundia, praesertim natura ipsa magistra et duce.Cum autem pulchritudinis duo genera sint, quorum in altero venustas sit, in altero dignitas, venustatem muliebrem ducere debemus, dignitatem virilem. Ergo et a forma removeatur omnis viro non dignus ornatus, et huic simile vitium in gestu motuque caveatur. Nam et palaestrici motus sunt saepe odiosiores, et histrionum non nulli gestus ineptiis non vacant, et in utroque genere quae sunt recta et simplicia, laudantur. (…) Adhibenda praeterea munditia est non odiosa neque exquisita nimis, tantum quae fugiat agrestem et inhumanam neglegentiam. Eadem ratio est habenda vestitus, in quo, sicut in plerisque rebus, mediocritas optima est." – Cic. *Off.*, 1.128-130.

is hardly ever inappropriate and does not need to be limited – it is *venustas* that requires moderation. Nevertheless, if used responsibly, the feminine charm proves worthy; more than that – the masculine together with the feminine is better than the masculine alone. Together they form a picture of a cultural, charming gentleman, who does not lose any of his dignity. In this new setting, Cicero emerges as a personification of the searched ideal. In the perspective he presents, it becomes clear that those criticising him for his feminine qualities are evidently too crude, too far away on the masculinity spectrum, while those criticised for the same by Cicero are too far to the other side. Providing examples of the more feminine public figures is essential for Cicero to prove that he is in fact appropriately distant from the extreme.

The duality of masculine and feminine refers not only to social conduct, but more particularly also to oratory practice and literary style, as in the above-mentioned passage by Quintilian. The qualities for which Cicero was criticised there include superfluous style, excess of repetitions, pointless witticism and fractured composition.[23] All these fall under category of emotional speech – described by Maud W. Gleason as the predominantly feminine trait in oratory performance.[24] She also notes some physical attributes, such as high voice and abundant gestures, associated with emotionality and femininity alike. These are precisely the characteristics Cicero is aiming at when he presents the mistakes and transgressions of other orators – such as the weak and soft movements of Sextus Titius that even inspired a parodic dance of a sort.[25] John Dugan presents yet another context in which the opposition of masculinity and femininity appears in Cicero's writings. He suggests that it overlaps with that of Stoicism and Epicureanism. Stoicism would stand for self-control and dignity, and therefore masculinity, Epicureanism for emotionality and pleasure-seeking – femininity.[26] Using this connection, Cicero reinvents the male virtue in a philosophical setting. One of the examples Dugan evokes is the critique of Crassus' emotional speech in *De Oratore*, where he passionately arguments that the senate should serve the people. Cicero's character Antonius points

---

[23] Quint., *Inst.*, 12.10.12.
[24] M. W. Gleason, *Making Men: Sophists and Self-Presentation in Ancient Rome*, pp. 103–130.
[25] Cic., *Brut.*, 225.
[26] J. Dugan, *Making a New Man, Ciceronian Self-Fashioning in the Rhetorical Works*, pp. 143–145.

out Crassus' weakness, affection and focus on the bodily experiences (*voluptatem corporis doloremque*), that made him forget that the senate's primary role is to guide and govern the people.[27] "(...) Antonius expands and unpacks the gender associations in the claim that Crassus is violating *virtus* – the abstraction of manliness that becomes translated within Stoicism to a philosophical conception of moral excellence – with a denunciation of Epicurean hedonism."[28] Such an interpretation suggests a significant difference from the position expressed by Caesar and Cato. Here, there is a clear distinction between the two kinds of philosophy – one that strengthens the mind, and one that weakens it. The general rules remain quite the same as presented in *Pro Archia* – it is the focus on emotions and pleasure that is feminising, and there exists a way of using the goods of culture that is not only proper for a man, but also required to shape his *virtus*.[29] The shift in the perception of which qualities may be perceived as socially valuable and masculine is by no means all Cicero's doing, but he certainly played an active role therein. I have been focusing on showing the ways in which Cicero defended the value of foreign culture. However, as Claudia Moatti underlined in her book *The Birth of Critical Thinking in Republican Rome*, he

[27] "Quod si ea probarentur in populis atque in civitatibus, quis tibi, Crasse, concessisset, clarissimo viro et amplissimo et principi civitatis, ut illa diceres in maxima contione tuorum civium, quae dixisti? 'Eripite nos ex miseriis, eripite ex faucibus eorum, quorum crudelitas nisi nostro sanguine non potest expleri; nolite sinere nos cuiquam servire, nisi vobis universis, quibus et possumus et debemus.' Omitto miserias, in quibus, ut illi aiunt, vir fortis esse non potest; omitto faucis, ex quibus te eripi vis, ne iudicio iniquo exsorbeatur sanguis tuus, quod sapienti negant accidere posse: servire vero non modo te, sed universum senatum, cuius tum causam agebas, ausus es dicere? Potestne virtus, Crasse, servire istis auctoribus, quorum tu praecepta oratoris facultate complecteris? Quae et semper et sola libera est, quaeque, etiam si corpora capta sint armis aut constricta vinculis, tamen suum ius atque omnium rerum impunitam libertatem tenere debeat. Quae vero addidisti, non modo senatum servire posse populo, sed etiam debere, quis hoc philosophus tam mollis, tam languidus, tam enervatus, tam omnia ad voluptatem corporis doloremque referens probare posset, senatum servire populo, cui populus ipse moderandi et regendi sui potestatem quasi quasdam habenas tradidisset?" – Cic., *De Orat.*, 1.225-226.

[28] J. Dugan, *op. cit.*, pp. 143-144.

[29] "(...) Rufus' defence, lacking ornament of any sort, was an account of the truth itself that failed to move the jurors, to whom Antonius refers with scorn. Rufus maintains his masculine objectivity by refusing to use such abject tactics. Like his model Socrates he retains his self-mastery at the docks and refuses any feminizing defence. Antonius relates that Socrates rejected Lysias' offer of a speech of defence on the ground that such a speech would be as effeminate as wearing Sicyonian slippers." – J. Dugan, op. cit., 145; cf. Cic., *De Orat.*, 1.231.

definitely did not want things to go too far – as he himself stressed in the passages of *De Officiis* discussed above. He too stood guard over the Roman values, even if he interpreted them differently than Cato. Meanwhile on some levels

> (...) Roman society was manifesting plenty of signs of this desire for novelty that seemed to bring the old values and the very status of tradition into question: the revolutionary philosophy of Lucretius, for instance, and the new-wave poetry of Catullus, Calvus and Cinna, all of them recently Romanised Italians and natives of Cisalpine Gaul, who in the 50s championed an aesthetics of frivolity and light poetry (*nugae*) that stood in stark contrast to Roman *gravitas*.[30]

An overly light sense of humour is one of Cicero's characteristics that Quintilian named as inappropriate for a man. Cicero does not wish to have the wit of his speech mistaken with the novel *nugae*. His style is influenced by *auctoritas* of the old Romans. He is aware that "Rome, which, according to Tacitus, was a traditionalist society that 'exalted the past,' maintained a limited 'temporal horizon.' If there was any place for novelty in it (...) it was, in the view of the elite at least, kept under control by respect of the ancient values."[31] *Gravitas* was one of the fundamental Roman values. Cicero valued humour, but in his account it had to serve *gravitas*. Cicero devotes chapters 216-290 of the second book of *De Oratore* to the appropriateness of humor. These passages are known as *excursus de ridiculis*. There Cicero refers to examples of dignified Roman citizens who skilfully used subtle jokes with no harm to their *gravitas*. He calls on their *auctoritas* in order to place his own wit in a worthy company. Brian Krostenko makes fascinating observations about Cicero's language in *De Oratore*. One of the points he makes is about Cicero's use of the word *lepos*, particularly in *excursus de ridiculis*. Cicero introduces new meanings to it, using it in a novel sense of "elegant, sophisticated wit." In spite of different – often negative – connotations the word brings in other contexts,[32] here it is definitely positive. It is a word that Cicero wishes to

[30]   C. Moatti, *The Birth of Critical Thinking in Republican Rome*, p. 39.
[31]   Ibidem, p. 38.
[32]   Krostenko stresses the fact that the adjective *lepidus* is still used in the negative sense by Cicero, regardless of the new meaning he added to the noun *lepos*. E.g. Cic., *Cat.*, 2.23: "hi pueri tam lepidi ac delicati non solum amare et amari neque saltare et cantare sed etiam sicas vibrare et spargere venena didicerunt."

mean a kind of humour fit for a gentleman, like the Roman statesmen he refers to. Krostenko suggests that Cicero longs for an equivalent for the Greek χάρις (charm, grace), and χάρις is what he means by his *lepos*.

> Ciceronian *lepos* is often concomitant to, and implicitly produced by, education and culture. Inside the rhetorica and out, Cicero connects *lepos* to *suavitas*, *urbanitas* and *humanitas*, all of which in one way or another have to do with the cultural standards of the urban elite. Caesar Strabo, to whom the discussion of humour in *De Oratore* is assigned, is elsewhere described as "paragon of culture, wit, pleasantness, and charm" (*specimen fuisse humanitatis salis, suavitatis leporis, Tusc.* 5.55). *Lepos* may also find itself in the company of words describing education and learning. Cicero's assignation of *lepos* to Stoic dialectic accords with this use. When Cicero attacks Epicurus for lacking *lepos* (N.D. 2.74 [...]), Cicero means that he lacks the wit, grace, and humour of Socratic dialectic.[33]

Through his apology of *cultus, humanitas, venustas* and *lepos*, Cicero replaces the accents in the common understanding of masculinity. Art and literature do not weaken the mind on their own, he shows. They may even strengthen it, if used properly. Only a frivolous use of culture – focused on pleasure and involving neglect of obligations to the state – should be looked down upon. In Cicero's account, emotional restraint is the key quality of a truly admirable man – what keeps him objective, reasonable and morally good. A study of literature and philosophy that is not focused on pleasure is a way of becoming that ideal gentleman. It can cause the opposite of what Caesar and Cato think *cultus* and *humanitas* do to the mind – it can strengthen it. "Philosophy heals the soul, takes away vain anxieties, frees from desires, drives out the fear" (*efficit hoc philosophia: medetur animis, inanes sollicitudines detrahit, cupiditatibus liberat, pellit timores*).[34] In Cicero's view it is in fact the fundament of the Roman – male – virtue.

---

[33]   B. Krostenko, op. cit., pp. 212–213.

[34]   "nam efficit hoc philosophia: medetur animis, inanes sollicitudines detrahit, cupiditatibus liberat, pellit timores. sed haec eius vis non idem potest apud omnis: tum valet multum, cum est idoneam complexa naturam. fortis enim non modo fortuna adiuvat, ut est in vetere proverbio, sed multo magis ratio, quae quibusdam quasi praeceptis confirmat vim fortitudinis. " – Cic., *Tusc.*, 2.11.

Source texts

(all the translations done by the paper's author)
Caesar, *De Bello Gallico.*
Cicero: *Pro Archia; Brutus; De Officiis; De Oratore; Tusculanae Disputationes.*
Plutarch, *Cato; Cicero.*
Quintilian, *Institutio Oratoria.*

Studies

Albrecht von M., *Cicero's Style*, Brill, Leiden–Boston 2003.

Berry D. H., *Literature and Persuasion in Cicero's Pro Archia* [in:] *Cicero the Advocate*, J. Powell, J. Paterson (eds.), Oxford University Press, Oxford 2004.

Dugan J. R., *Making a New Man: Ciceronian Self-Fashioning in the Rhetorical Works*, Oxford University Press, Oxford 2005.

Gleason M. W., *Making Men: Sophists and Self-Presentation in Ancient Rome*, Princeton University Press, Princeton 1995.

Gruen E. S., *Culture and National Identity in the Republican Rome*, Cornell University Press, Ithaca 1992.

Habinek T. N., *The Politics of Roman Empire: Writing, Identity and Empire in Ancient Rome*, Princeton University Press, Princeton 1998.

Krostenko B., *Cicero, Catullus and the Language of Social Performance*, University of Chicago Press, Chicago 2001.

McKendrick P., *The Philosophical Books of Cicero*, Palgrave Macmillan, London 1989.

Moatti C., *The Birth of Critical Thinking in Republican Rome*, J. Lloyd (trans.), Cambridge University Press, Cambridge 2015.

AGNIESZKA GONDOR-WIERCIOCH
ⓘ http://orcid.org/0000-0002-8849-0942

KILL THE SAVAGE, SAVE THE MAN – JAMES WELCH'S CHRONICLE OF NATIVE AMERICAN HISTORY

Abstract: The article discusses the way in which contemporary Native American author James Welch reconstructs the history of the Blackfoot Nation. Welch manages to create a counter-history of the U.S. by creating a hybrid discourse; he presents the inner perspective of his characters by providing them with a language that is a mixture of English and Pikuni borrowings. Additionally, Welch addresses the theme of male dignity when he deconstructs popular Indian stereotypes and fills the void with complex multidimensional Native American characters. The article focuses on two historical novels – *Fools Crow* and *The Heartsong of Charging Elk* – that rely to a large extent on historical data and aim to reconstruct the Blackfoot worldview. The main aim of the narrative is to reconstruct ethnohistory and search for a hybrid form reinforced through storytelling techniques, mythological references and magical realist strategies. The article refers to the theoretical frame proposed by critics and academics such as, among others, Louis Owens, Arnold Krupat, Ron McFarland and Catherine Rainwater.

Keywords: contemporary Native American literature, transculturation, counter-history

There is no denying that masculine characters are extremely important in the literary vision of James Welch. Just like other contemporary Native American writers, through literature Welch wanted to represent not some vague "Indian" culture, but the particularity of his background – Blackfoot heritage. In order to complete this difficult task, he had to start by deconstructing one of the most widespread stereotypes of American Indians, i.e. the Savage Warrior of the Plains. The Blackfeet had all the desired attributes to conform to this cliché because they lived nomadic lives on the plains and they were defeated at the time of the so-called Indian Wars. With the defeat, the Blackfeet joined the ranks of the indigenous who had been stripped of their cultural differences and branded "Vanishing Indians." There is no denying that Edward Curtis' sepia photos contributed greatly to this popular image of Native Americans who transformed from bloodthirsty primitives into romantic characters doomed to perish. The Western movies consolidated these stereotypes in mass imagination and it was only in the late 1960s that Native American Renaissance authors started to seriously challenge these static images.

In my paper I would like to argue that Welch not only shattered the stereotypes but managed to create literary works that have universal value for both Native American and non-Native-American critics and readers even though he wrote his novels in English. In order to explain how Welch managed to reconstruct a lost identity through a historical novel in which he emphasised the perspective of male characters who are far from Western movies images of Indian warriors, I have decided to play on the infamous motto of the Carlise boarding school "Kill the Indian, save the Man" whose purpose was exactly the contrary of Welch's mission.[1] Just like boarding schools deprived Native American of their culture and history, Welch ensured they regained it through his literary achievement. Similarly to Louise Erdrich, Leslie Marmon Silko or Sherman Alexie, he created fiction that explores the counter-history of the periphery that not only provides an alternative model against the official history of the U.S., but also inspires interesting structural solutions and invokes indigenous worldviews. Before I present Welch's most important historical novels – *Fools Crow* and *The Heartsong of Charging Elk* – let me first refer briefly to his biography and ethnic background because without it his works remain beyond the reach of non-Indian readers.

James Welch was born in Browning, Montana and this state became the setting for the majority of his works. His father was a Blackfoot, his mother a Gros Ventre, and James spent his early years in Blackfeet and Fort Belknap reservations. Later James Welch moved to Missoula and studied at the University of Montana. During his studies, poet Richard Hugo advised him to find inspiration in his roots and in this way Welch's first collection of poetry *Riding the Earthboy 40* was born and published in 1971. After 7 years, Welch turned to fiction and published his first

---

[1]   I also owe the title to Ward Churchill's *Kill the Indian, Save the Man: The Genocidal Impact of American Indian Residential Schools.*

novel – *Winter in the Blood* – which was well-received by readers and critics. His best work is *Fools Crow*, published in 1986 and considered the first Native American historical novel, in which Welch commemorated his great-grandmother whom he only knew through the stories told by his father. His last novel *The Heartsong of Charging Elk* (2000) brought him fame and awards in France.[2] Welch also wrote non-fiction, such as *Killing Custer* which retells the story of the battle of Little Bighorn from a Native American perspective. The book was a follow-up to the screenplay written by Welch for the Emmy winning documentary "Last Stand at Little Bighorn", so writing about history in novels as well as his individual awakening with regard to Blackfoot spirituality evolved into true historical challenges for Welch. As Welch himself explained it, recollecting one of the first Blackfoot ceremonies in which he participated: "As they made their way to the Medicine Lodge, a voice, high and distant, sang to the sun and it entered my bones as I was Blackfoot and changed forever. I remember."[3]

Welch's ethnic background is extremely important for the understanding of *Fools Crow*. The Blackfeet are among the best known Plains tribes and in the mainstream culture represent the essence of American Indians. As many other Native American cultures in the U.S. they were not homogenous as people but emerged as a confederation of smaller groups. The Blackfoot nation was created in 1855 as a result of a treaty between four tribes: Northern Blackfeet, Bloods, Piegans and Gros Ventre. The confederation ended when the group was defeated in the Marias river massacre in 1870 by the U.S. cavalry; afterwards the Blackfoot Nation had to follow a pattern typical for other tribes because they had to accept different forms of acculturation through boarding schools, living in reservations, losing their languages and history.[4] The novel *Fools Crow* tells the history of Blackfeet several decades before the massacre, but before I present the novel in detail, I would like to show a larger context for my analysis and interpretation.

As previously mentioned, Welch's works belong to the tradition of Native American literature and he therefore shares much in common with authors such as N. Scott Momaday, Louise Erdrich, Leslie Marmon Silko,

---

[2]   R. McFarland, *Understanding James Welch*.
[3]   M. J. Lupton, *Interview with James Welch*; N. Barry, *"A Myth to be Alive": James Welch's Fools Crow*, p. 3.
[4]   N. Barry, op. cit.

Sherman Alexie, to name just a few. All these writers believe that in order to be a Native American writer or poet one has to start from the deconstruction of stereotypes as harmful and omnipresent as Columbus' Indian, Rousseau's Noble Savage, Curtis' Vanishing Indian (Romantic fancy staged in front of the camera) and Hollywood's Indian Warrior and Squaw (primitive beasts not able to respond to the civilising impulses of the white man). Apart from the stereotypes, the main problem for Welch and other authors was to find his own language. Since only several Native American artists spoke tribal languages, English became the only medium that reflects to some extent the linguistic traditions of indigenous cultures. One of the most prevailing strategies was inserting words and phrases from Native American languages or introducing narrative devices typical for oral literature. There was also the question of the genre of prose, which turned out to be the Euro-American novel transformed by alterations inspired by Native American mythologies and storytelling techniques; this is how trickster novels or short story cycles were born in contemporary Native American fiction. Last, but not least, came the question of how to represent the Native American worldview and identity; for Welch, this quest began with reconstructing Blackfoot history. What is worth noticing is that, as in the case of other ethnic literatures, history enters Native American fictional worlds as a counter-history to the official historical discourse.

Before I embark on literary analysis and interpretation, I would like to remind the readers what influenced the misrepresentation of Native American men before their ambitious literary portraits appeared in the second half of the 20th century. Thomas King[5] addresses this issue thoroughly when he examines the policy towards indigenous people in Canada and the U.S. along with the impact of this policy on the way Native Americans have been perceived by the general public. As many other academics, King particularly emphasizes elements of colonial and neocolonial practice such as the numerous forceful relocations of Native American nations, allotment acts, obligatory boarding schools and termination policy. There is no place to discuss all of this abuse in detail, but I would like to concentrate for a moment on the boarding schools because they affected whole generations by ruining individuals and families. While it is true that nowadays the residents of many Native Americans reservations face poverty, violence as well as drug and alcohol abuse,

---

[5]   T. King, *The Inconvenient Indian. A Curious Account of Native People in North America.*

the public rarely associates these conditions with historical processes or events. King concludes that despite the fact that Canada is perceived as a country which values multiculturalism more, it always mirrored the hostile and unjust policy against Native Americans that the USA had introduced. The writer points out that the Canadian government usually introduced the same legal acts that excluded Indians from democracy but several decades later than the U.S. government. The argument supporting this conclusion might be found in Termination and Relocations Acts that Canadians issued in the 1950s and 60s even though it was clear that similar acts introduced in the U.S. had been disastrous. King enumerates about 1,500 treaties signed between Europeans and Indians, emphasizing that when treaty signing was eliminated by law in 1871 in the U.S., the policy was initiated in Canada. As a result of this shameful practice (the treaties were never observed because Europeans and later Americans and Canadians always needed more land), Indians, as King explains, became property of the governments ("not slaves, more like furniture"[6]) because they gradually lost the ownership of their land. In popular view, the Indians were reduced to the status of children, not mature enough to manage their own affairs.

Coming back to the boarding schools, King does not see any difference in the inhumane practices that were implemented by school authorities in Canada and the U.S. The contrast was cosmetic; in Canada the schools were called "residential" in the U.S. "boarding"; in the former case they were usually run by Catholic and in the latter by Protestant clergy. The "solution to the Indian problem" was strikingly similar and strikingly atrocious. There is no point in creating a competition regarding who was crueler or who started earlier. As King observes, such schools were obligatory for all children from 6 to 15, often punishable by prison for parents, usually hundreds of miles from home. Children were completely stripped of their identity; physical punishment was rife. According to the national surveys conducted in the 1930s in the U.S. and the 1960s in Canada, 50% of children in residential schools in the U.S. and Canada lost their lives to disease, malnutrition, neglect and abuse.[7] In 1986 the Catholic Church expressed regret, followed by other churches in the 1990s. In 2009 Benedict XVI expressed sorrow, but never apologised. King also acknowledges the steps taken by government

[6]   Ibidem, p. 81.
[7]   Ibidem, p. 85.

authorities. In 2008 Canadian Prime Minister Stephen Harper made an apology in the House of Commons to the representatives of the Natives and it was broadcast on national television. The U.S. government never apologised. Barack Obama passed an official apology resolution but never said sorry publicly. Still he issued a document that expressed remorse for the Removal Act, massacres and the General Allotment Act. In conclusion King writes that even though Canadian official apology was a better step as far as educating the public was concerned, the same Prime Minister earlier officially said that Canadians "have no history of colonialism," so the overall impression is that since nobody took responsibility, there is still place for paternalistic intervention.[8]

The results of such treatment of Native American issues always affected the way in which the public perceived Native Americans and there is no denying that Hollywood was responsible for spreading harmful stereotypes through the mass production of westerns. I do not want to overgeneralize that every western is a misrepresentation of Native American cultures but the majority of them definitely offer the public Indian caricatures. Before I present the observations of Thomas King which I consider particularly insightful, I would like to remind the readers that Europeans have also contributed to this misrepresentations not only through Italian spaghetti westerns or German Winnetou stories but by the Polish Indian novels popular in the communist Poland. All these phenomena might be better understood by the desire for Dead Indians and dislike for Live Indians that King elaborates on. Dead Indians are the best recognized tribe in the U.S., writes King because the average American likes westerns and folklore festivals and he/she has expectations of what Indians he/she should meet there. As King explains: "For Native People, the distinction between Dead Indians and Live Indians is almost impossible to maintain. But North America doesn't have a problem. All it has to do is hold the two Indians up to the light. Dead Indians are dignified, noble, silent, suitably garbed. And dead. Live Indians are invisible, unruly, disappointing. And breathing. One is a romantic reminder of a heroic but fictional past. The other is simply an unpleasant, contemporary surprise."[9] His lecture on the differences between dead and live Indians would not be complete without King's remark that "In order to maintain the cult and sanctity of the Dead Indian, North America has

8   Ibidem, p. 113.
9   Ibidem, p. 66.

decided that live Indians living today cannot be genuine Indians."[10] It is obvious that the status of all unreal Indians is deeply rooted in popular culture myths and complete ignorance of historical facts. I would like to argue that, for this particular reason, history is a such an important frame of reference for contemporary Native American writers such as James Welch. Their starting point must be the deconstruction of stereotypes and the struggle against ignorance, just as always one of their goals is restoring dignity.

Looking at the works of Welch, I decided to use the theoretical frame proposed by the scholars such as Louis Parkinson Zamora, Arnold Krupat and Louis Owens. Zamora wrote some important articles in which the concept of America's "buried past" was introduced in order to emphasize the common ground between the American and Mexican contexts.[11] In his article, Zamora compared three novels – *House of Breath* by William Goyen, *Pedro Paramo* by Juan Rulfo and *Recollections of Things to Come* by Elena Garro – which present counter-histories of the colonization of America told by the communities of the dead who try to reach the living be means of magical realist. Although Welch does not introduce dead people as characters in his novels he also reconstructs ethno-histories of communities torn apart and shows alternative histories of colonization. Additionally, Welch uses magical realism in *Fools Crow* in order to introduce a Blackfoot myth into his historical narrative.

Another critical frame can be found in the writing of Arnold Krupat who concentrated on the differences between the ways in which Native Americans and Euro-Americans perceive history. Krupat stresses the need for mix-blood writers such as Welch to create a hybrid discourse out of two different perspectives emphasizing two different time patterns: chronological and cyclical. Native American perspective does not rely so much on historical facts but incorporates myths into a historical narrative that help to expose certain timeless patterns and portray man not as an active perpetrator of events, but as part of a sacred hoop whose main goal is to ensure harmony with nature, universe and the world of the ancestors. Krupat warns against dismissing this outlook on the basis of being not scientific enough because without it Native Americans cannot be Native Americans and when their history is told

[10] Ibidem, p. 64.
[11] L. P. Zamora, *Magical Romance/Magical Realism: Ghosts in U.S. and Latin American Fiction.*

exclusively in a Euro-American way it becomes a false representation. Native Americans as mix-bloods in the majority of cases must negotiate between different historical models heading towards dialogic transcultural perspective.[12] Louis Owens also recognizes this need in the context of postcolonial studies as his analysis of *Fools Crow* indicates.[13]

The theme of history reconstruction as well as the strategies that Welch introduces are interconnected with the characters who inhabit the fictional space. There is no denying that James Welch, next to Sherman Alexie, is among the authors who paid special attention to male characters. What is particularly important for both Welch and Alexie is to counteract the impact of the omnipresent stereotypes of American Indians such as Noble Savage, Indian Warrior and Vanishing Indian that were white fantasies about Native American men. The difference between Alexie and Welch is that Alexie did not focused so much on history reconstruction but centered on the psychological consequences that these stereotypes cause for contemporary reservation and urban Indians. Welch started from a similar theme in his novel *The Death of Jim Loney*,[14] but he abandoned it in his later works because instead of showing the void that the stereotypes created in the identity of contemporary Native Americans, he decided to root their identity in concrete history which could help them to regain their lost male dignity. *Fools Crow* is a novel in which he achieves his aim, not only because he managed to populate it with credible male characters, but for the reason that he created impressive epic scenery very far from the historical renditions of American Indians produced by, for example, James Fenimore Cooper or less ambitious writers such as Karol May.

Before I concentrate on the more detailed interpretation of Welch's historical novels, I would like to stress that neither Alexie nor Welch excluded women from their fiction; nor did they insist that history was created only by men. Women are vital part of their fictional worlds but they do not primarily focus on a feminist perspective such as Louise Erdrich, Linda Hogan and particularly Leslie Marmon Silko who comes from the matrilineal culture of Laguna Pueblo.

Fools Crow is a story of a hero coming from the band of Lone Eaters (one of 12 subgroups of the Pikuni clan, a sub-group of the Blackfoot

[12] A. Krupat, *American Histories, Native American Narratives.*
[13] L. Owens, *Other Destinies: Understanding the American Indian Novel.*
[14] J. Welch, *The Death of Jim Loney.*

nation), named White Man's Dog who goes through Native American rites of passage and becomes Fools Crow (because he managed to fool Blackfeet's enemies the Crows, in a battle). Fools Crow matures in the novel and becomes a visionary and protector of his people in the difficult times of the second half of the 19th century when Napikwans (white settlers and soldiers) threaten the territory of Pikuni. Additionally, some young Pikuni warriors such as Owl Child, raid Napikwans mercilessly and provoke military confrontations that endanger the whole tribe. In fact Old Child's band kills a white man they accidentally encounter, which later leads to the Marais River massacre in which hundreds of Pikuni are killed by the white invaders. Fools Crow sees the demise of his people in a dream but does not give up and till the end of the novel ensures the continuity of the Blackfoot ceremonies.

The biggest achievement of Welch is the realist style of the novel which is never sentimental and devoid of romantic stereotypes typical for the fiction of, for example, James Fenimore Cooper.[15] How does he achieve this? First of all, Welch made sure that his novel is grounded in historical data. Starting from autobiographical stories and ending by including figures and events from Native American history, Welch is consistent in creating a complex picture of the history of two cultures clashed in a tragic conflict. This attempt to represent both sides of the conflict is connected with Welch's family background.[16] As for the Native American side, his great-grandmother Red Paint who survived the Marais River massacre is present in the novel in the person of Fools Crow's wife and as for the white side, Malcolm Clark, a relative of Welch who was killed by Blackfeet in 1869, is a part of the novel under his original name (he gets killed by Old Child's band). Louis Owens notices that the whole plot of *Fools Crow* is based on historical material that can be verified. For example, the novel records two epidemics that Pikuni went through in the 19th century, the names of the chiefs such as Heavy Runner, Little Dog, Mountain Chief and Big Lake are names of true historical chiefs, similarly to the names of white protagonists such as Joe Kipp and Malcolm Clark. The main source of inspiration for Welch were *Blackfoot Lodge Tales* by George Bird Grinnel, a 19th century chronicle of the Blackfeet which not only provided Welch with historical facts but also the language.

---

[15] David Treuer does not agree with this interpretation as he explains in his controversial *Native American Fiction – A User's Manual*.

[16] L. Owens, op. cit.

Sometimes Welch manipulated historical material a little, albeit rarely, like, for example, in the case of Blackfoot band of renegades who killed Malcolm Clark; such band really existed but the name of its leader was unknown; in Welch's novel its leader is Old Child; historically it was a name of a successful Blackfoot farmer. Welch also reconstructed the historical Marais River Massacre, but the chief Heavy Runner who really died in it, survives in Welch's novel. Similarly Welch reconstructs the historical scene in which his great-grandmother participated; historically Red Paint was one of the survivors of the massacre who informed other bands what had happened. In the novel the scene is recreated when Fools Crow meets the survivors and talks to the woman modelled on Welch's great-grandmother, but her name is not Red Paint, because Welch gave this name to Fools Crow's wife. There are more historical scenes and characters in the novel, but it is enough to mention these to prove that history is as important for him as myth.

It is not only important what Welch included, but how, so the question of genre is worth introducing. The majority of critics agree[17] that Welch wrote the best ever Native American historical novel, which is a good example of hybridization because apart from historical realism Welch incorporated into his work a mythic dimension through magical realist conventions. Blackfoot mythology appears mostly in Fools Crow's dreams and visions and does not affect the credibility of the historical narrative. Owens also notices that:

> By re-imagining, or re-remembering the traditional Blackfoot world, Welch attempts to recover the center – to revitalize the "myths of identity and authenticity" – and thus reclaim the possibility of a coherent identity for himself and all contemporary Blackfoot people, that which was denied to Jim Loney.[18]

How exactly does Welch achieve authentic transcultural American/Blackfoot narrative? First of all, through the language which is English but full of Blackfoot calques such as: "bighorns" for "the buffalo" or "the above ones" for "the gods". The world of Pikuni is described from the inside in simple but not primitive English combined with words and phrases

---

[17] Except Treuer, but his position has been criticised by important writers and academics such as Arnold Krupat for example
[18] L. Owens, op. cit., p.157.

that are direct translation of certain Blackfoot concepts and ideas. The effect is as in this quote:

> White Man's Dog watched Seven Persons rise into the night sky above Chief Mountain. Above, The Star-that-stands-still waited for the others to gather around him. White Man's Dog felt Cold Maker's breath in his face, but it looked as though he would keep the clouds in Always Winter Land tonight. He was only warning the Pikunis that his season was near.[19]

In this way Welch expands the discourse of the novel creating the language the Blackfeet might have used if they had spoken English. Owens notices that through this strategy Welch' third person narrator takes control over the picture of the American colonization and makes English carry the burden of the foreign language by forcing the English readers to travel through a world that is mentally alien.[20] The Blackfeet speak from the center and the Napikwan remain on the periphery. If the language is the medium which exposes the hierarchical structure of power, then the power belongs to the Blackfeet in the novel. What is also important is that Welch does not idealize the Blackfoot culture; some critics (e.g. Nora Barry)[21] notice that even though the story of Fools Crow and his wife has an epic dimension and these characters at times look and behave like epic heroes (Fools Crow communicates with the gods and performs unusual feats, also functioning in some kind of mythic time and becoming a true hero who protects the Blackfoot nation from its rise to fall both in everyday life and on a supernatural level) there are also weak characters in the novel. Thus Welch creates Blackfoot characters who are undeniably human and they function as counterparts to the heroic figures of Fools Crow and Red Paint. Such characters are Yellow Kidney, Fools Crow's father-in-law, or Running Fisher, his brother who cheats their father by seducing his youngest wife Kills-Close-to-the-Lake. There is also Fast Horse who is driven by sick ambition and betrays Lone Eaters by joining Owl Child's band of villains. Welch's characters are not only courageous and protective as Fools Crow, but also cruel, vindictive, blinded by competition and often failing to live according to the moral values of the group that Fools Crow follows. The

[19] J. Welch, *Fools Crow*, p. 5.
[20] L. Owens, op. cit., p. 158
[21] N. Barry, op. cit.

conclusion might be that being Native American before contact with the white man had little in common with being naïve as a child. As critic Ron McFarland puts it: "The nobility of the Indian is no less stereotype than the savagery. Welch insists that his Native American be human."[22] Thus there is no trace of macho in Welch's male characters. According to Octavio Paz (*Labyrinth of Solitude*),[23] macho is a mask behind which weak and frustrated men hide themselves because they are too cowardly to act and stand for their values. Welch's men always face the consequences and take responsibility and they listen to others, particularly women. The proof might be observed in the magical realist motif of the relationship between Fools Crow and the mythic women that guides him.

The question of magical realism is also important and it divides the critics, some claiming that there is no magical realism in the novel because for Welch's characters everything they experience is true (Owens' position). I agree with those critics who notice magical realism in the novel, because I see many similarities between the way in which Welch incorporates magic into the realistic texture of his novel and the methods explored by classical magical realist novelists in Latin American tradition. What Welch has in common with writers such as Alejo Carpentier, Juan Rulfo, Gabriel García Márquez and Rosario Castellanos is that he erases the boundaries between the real and the imaginary, allowing a double interpretation of events. Fantastic events occur mostly in dreams and visions, so we cannot be sure if supernatural beings are only a part of Fools Crow's consciousness or they become a part of the reality in which the characters live. In this way Welch complicates the picture of the Pikuni reality and makes his readers more aware of the contrast between his Native American and white characters. Critic Ron McFarland also notices it:

> One appealing attribute of the novel is the deftness with which Welch handles such border-crossings between the mundane and the spiritual, the effect of which on the reader is similar to that of magic realist fiction in the vein of Gabriel García Márquez, Luisa Valenzuela, and other Latin American writers.[24]

[22]   Ron McFarland, op. cit., p. 121.
[23]   O. Paz, *Labyrinth of Solitude*.
[24]   Ron McFarland, op. cit., p. 116.

Hans Bak calls it "tribal realism,"[25] to stress the role this type of realism plays in exposing the intricacies of the ethnic context. This critic also addresses the controversy around Welch connected with his status as a mix-blood writer. Together with Louise Erdrich and Sherman Alexie, Welch was attacked by Elisabeth Cook-Lynn for sacrificing the Indian vision for the sake of pleasing a non-Indian audience by, first of all, choosing non-Indian formal strategies, typical for a Euro-American novel. Bak agrees that in *Fools Crow* the genre is Euro-American, but he calls for not falling into the trap of essentialism, as he says:

> Instead of faulting the novel for being incongruously accomodationist, one might more properly appreciate Welch's achievement by considering the degree to which *Fools Crow* manages to bridge the traditional boundaries of Western and tribal generic and linguistic conventions, in order to create a new cross-cultural and transgeneric middle-space, where realism and tribalism are negotiated dialectically and made to work on each other in a playful and creative fashion.[26]

White characters do not have access to the supernatural dimension of reality but they are not portrayed as villains, but rather as outsiders. Just as Pikuni are at home in Welch's novel because they recognize the elements of nature with which they live in harmony in the majority of cases, Napikwans function in the landscape that is empty for them and their perception of the world exposes their alienation like in the quote:

> The rolling prairies were as vast and empty as a pale ocean, and the sky stretched forever, sometimes blue, sometimes slate. The few small groups of mountains, like islands in this sea of yellow swells, only seems to emphasize its vastness. In the winter, when snow covered the land and lay heavy in the bottoms, the man was filled with foreboding dreams of an even larger isolation.[27]

The second historical novel that is also worth mentioning, because Welch reinforces his bond with history within, is *The Heartsong of Charging Elk* where he presents the story of a Lakota Sioux Indian Charging Elk

[25]   H. Bak, *The Art of Hybridization – James Welch's Fools Crow*.
[26]   Ibidem, p. 35.
[27]   J. Welch, *Fools Crow*, pp. 289–290.

who got lost in France during Buffalo Bill Show's Tour around Europe in the second half of the 19th century. Just as in the case of *Fools Crow* Welch was inspired by a true story; two times running during his reading tours he met young Native Americans whose ancestors had traveled with Buffalo Bill and got lost in Europe. The fictional story of Charging Elk is similarly to the story of Fools Crow grounded in a verifiable historical context. Gradually we learn about the blows aimed at Native American cultures in the background of the novel, for example:

> But that spring Crazy Horse led the weary, ragged people to Fort Robinson and Red Cloud Agency. They surrounded their horses and weapons, everything but their garments, cooking utensils, and lodges. The piece of paper that the leader marked was dated May 6, 1877. Four months later, in the Moon of the Black Calf, Crazy Horse was killed by the soldiers with the help of some of his own people.[28]

The readers are familiarized with the defeats that Lakotas and other cultures suffered during the so-called Indian Wars (the most conspicuous is the Wounded Knee massacre Elk experiences through a nightmare). Meanwhile the main character is trying to live on his own in 19th century Marseille where he not only learns some French and earns his living but falls in love with a prostitute, commits a murder and does his time in prison. Upon release, he also becomes a farmer and marries a French girl. The tragedy of Charging Elk is not so much his assimilation, because he finally finds peace with his new French family, but the fact that he cannot return to the U.S. In fact, Welch was planning to write a sequel in which Charging Elk comes back home but he died of cancer in 2004.

As for his last novel, critics agree (e.g. Sarah Fergusson) that the story was inspired by the memoirs of a famous Lakota Black Elk, recorded by the white poet, John Neihardt in 1932. Black Elk also got lost during the Buffalo Bill Tour, not in Marseille, but in Paris. He also learned some French and experienced a different vision through which he became aware with the fate of his people in America. Similarly to *Fools Crow,* in this novel Welch also uses Blackfoot calques such as "Greasy Grass" indicating the battlefield of Little Bighorn or "heartsong" which is a "deathsong" sang on special occasions (also by Black Elk). For me the most interesting parts of the novel are connected with Elk's perception

---

[28] Idem, *The Heartsong of Charging Elk*, p. 12.

of European culture. Just as in *Fools Crow*, the white world is on the outside presented as something alien, sometimes funny, sometimes repulsive. This is particularly visible in a scene in which Elk describes the Nativity Scene with Mary, Joseph, Jesus, shepherds and the Magi, but this is what we infer, reading between the lines, because, what Elk sees is something different. The same refers to our association with the picture; where we see Christmas, Elk sees an exotic setting, as absurd as the European political system in which he sees no traces of progress and civilisation but randomness and chaos, as in the quote:

> Charging Elk saw a group of people standing before a big window. They were talking and gesturing and pointing at various groups of small figures. Some of them were animals – cattle, sheep, and pigs. Charging Elk remembered it because he had never smelled such a sharp, sour odor. It seemed to ride with him for many miles afterward. (...)

In the middle of the window, he saw a group of figures that seemed to be apart from the others and quite a bit larger. Three bearded men in different dress stood or kneeled. One had a tall cloth wrapped around his head. Charging Elk recognized this figure. At the show in Paris, at the foot of the naked iron tree they called the Eiffel Tower, he had seen real men wear these big hats. They came from even farther to the east where they rode the long-necked, big-humped beasts that he had first seen in a pen at the exhibition. They had looked hot and ugly, but when he touched the chewing muzzle of one, he was surprised how soft and pleasant it felt. Sees Twice told him that the Eiffel Tower had been built so the French could honor their five generations of freedom from cruel kings. All the surrounding buildings and fountains and gardens were part of this honoring ceremony. He said the white men of America had a similar honoring. They had defeated a cruel king many years before. Featherman had wondered aloud if all kings were cruel, but Seese Twice couldn't answer that. He only knew that the Grandmother England was kind. Maybe only woman kings were good to their people.[29]

In this passage it is worth noticing that Welch invokes untypical associations for the Christmas scene that is so familiar to representatives of Western Culture. Both non-Indian readers and assimilated Indians have to make effort to decipher the story behind the description. What

[29]   Ibidem, pp. 40-41.

is also important, is a subtle sense of humor that allows us to laugh at both Indians and Europeans. The Indians are funny because they associate the Nativity Scene with a pig smell, they do not know the word for camel and perceive the powerful Queen Victoria as a nice grandmother. But if we continue reading we find out that Charging Elk has no idea why the blacks in that scene have huge red mouths, particularly that he had seen black men already and none of them had this feature. So not only is the Indian vision limited but the Non-Indian as well. Both novels, *Fools Crow* and *The Heartsong of the Charging Elk* are also proof that Welch was never interested in radical revisionism. Welch himself additionally made it clear in one of the interviews when he said: "I think it is becoming more and more acceptable to say 'Indians'. Those days of pain and so on are fading. People on reservations call each other Indians."[30]

Finally, I would like to emphasize that *The Heartsong of the Charging Elk,* similarly to *Fools Crow,* may help Native American men to regain their lost dignity. The main character reaches Europe as a part of a circus in which Native Americans were cast as clowns, savage clowns, caricatures of true American Indians. The Buffalo Bill Show indeed fulfilled the American and European dream of encountering the last "Savage Indian." This degradation and humiliation was even more painful when some indigenous performers realized that while they were ridiculing Native traditions, members of their tribes were being killed or forcefully relocated to reservations. Charging Elk tries to start a new life in Europe because he realizes there is no coming back. James Welch provides us with the inner perspective of his Lakota character to makes us realize how it felt to hide despair behind the mask of the clown and how much it cost to remove this mask and prove to be a man in a land that was alien and hostile. Even though the portrait of Charging Elk may seem too sentimental when compared to Fools Crow, Welch is consistent in constructing characters who find male dignity by facing the consequences of their actions and finding the courage to make their own decisions in dramatic historical circumstances when the homicide of Native American was justified by paternalistic allegations that saving the man goes with killing the Indian in him.

James Welch's achievement is even more striking if we compare it with that of James Fenimore Cooper who monopolized the history of white-Indian relations in literature for many decades using the same

[30]   M. J. Lupton, op. cit., p. 4.

genre of the historical novel. When one contrasts the historical visions of Cooper and Welch, one can discover that Cooper is not only guilty of creating stereotypes of Indians, but of manipulation of the historical data. One of the best historical accounts of Native American experience are the works by Peter Nabokov[31] and James Wilson[32] which definitely contribute to readers' better understanding of Welch's ethnohistorical quest and Cooper's Eurocentric fantasy. Although neither Nabokov nor Wilson refer to Welch, they shed light on important aspects of Native American history that has been silenced for decades. Especially Wilson's work is important in my opinion because it reconstructs the history later misrepresented by Cooper. It is the history of Woncus of the Mohegan tribe who was rejected by the Pequots in 1633 when he tried to become their chief. As revenge, Woncus cooperated with white settlers against the Pequots during the so-called Pequot wars. At that time the Pequot tribe led by their chief Sassacus sustained friendly relations with Massachusetts Bay colonists and were in conflict with Connecticut settlers directed by John Mason. Woncus chose Mason as his ally and when the two sides (the Pequots and the Connecticut settlers) decided to meet in battle, Woncus betrayed the location of the village where the Pequots had left their women and children. Then the white settlers and soldiers massacred the Pequot families and the warriors grieved so much that they lost the battle. Woncus became "a true Indian friend" of the whites even though his cruelty and appetite for human flesh (there is evidence that he was a cannibal) were widely known. As Wilson concludes in his history, centuries later, Woncus, the first of the Mohegans, called Uncas by the English, was chosen by James Fenimore Copper as a memorable Noble Savage of his novel, the last of the Mohicans.[33]

Nowhere in his historical novels was Welch tempted by this kind of fantasy, although writing a counter-history of the colonization of America is a revisionist task and one can easily understand the temptation to take revenge and expose the brutality of the white man more than the cruelty of the Indians. What is worth considering though, is why we trusted Fenimore Cooper as a historical writer for so long and why some readers and critics question the right of Native American authors to represent

---

[31] P. Nabokov, *Native American Testimony. A Chronicle of Indian-White Relations from Prophesy to the Present.*
[32] J. Wilson, *The Earth Shall Weep. A History of Native America.*
[33] Ibidem, p. 97.

their cultures just because their first language is English and they write novels instead of producing oral literature. The concept of transculturation gives the opportunity to acknowledge this right and change our way of thinking. Catherine Rainwater, refers to it when she summarizes the role contemporary Native American literature plays:

> (...) these writers thoroughly and systematically contest the western stereotypical notion that 'power and control (are) outside the range of the Indian imagination.' Their works also testify to the fact that the dominant discourse is always 'at risk of disruption' by contradictory statements formulated within the strictures of that same discourse. Unfolding within the strictures of Eurocentric written narratives, these texts nevertheless demand non-Eurocentric interpretations based on nonwestern worldviews. Thus the dominant discourse is readily 'counter-colonized' by 'subversive' semiotic practices that, in turn, become a part of the dominant discourse. Such counter-colonizing texts expand the Euro-American epistemological frame and facilitate the entry of other such texts – and their concomitant worldviews and 'realities' – into the dominant domain.[34]

Thus the role of the transcultural strategies is not merely to make space for Native American experience but also broaden non-Indian horizons.

BIBLIOGRAPHY

Bak H., *The Art of Hybridization – James Welch's Fools Crow*, "American Studies in Scandinavia", Vol. 27, 1995, pp. 33-47.

Barry N., *"A Myth to Be Alive": James Welch's Fools Crow*, "MELUS", Vol. 17, No. 1, 1991-1992, pp. 3-19.

Churchill W., *Kill the Indian, Save the Man: The Genocidal Impact of American Indian Residential Schools*, City Lights Bookstore, San Francisco 2004.

Fergusson S., *Europe and the Quest for Home in James Welch's The Heartsong of Charging Elk and Leslie Marmon's Gardens in the Dunes*, "Studies in American Indian Literatures", Summer 2006, pp. 34-53.

King T., *The Inconvenient Indian. A Curious Account of Native People in North America*, University of Minnesota Press, Minneapolis 2012.

Krupat A., *American Histories, Native American Narratives*. "Early American Literature", Vol. 30, 1995, pp. 165-172.

[34] C. Rainwater, *Dreams of Fiery Stars. The Transformations of Native American Fiction.*

Lupton M. J., *Interview with James Welch*, "American Indian Quaterly", Vol. 29, Nos. 1-2, 2005, pp. 198-203.

McFarland R., *Understanding James Welch*, University of South Carolina Press, Columbia 2000.

Nabokov P., *Native American Testimony. A Chronicle of Indian-White Relations from Prophesy to the Present*, Penguin Books, New York 1991.

Owens L., *Other Destinies: Understanding the American Indian Novel*, University of Oklahoma Press, Norman 1992.

Paz O., *Labyrinth of Solitude*, Grove Press, New York 1961.

Rainwater C., *Dreams of Fiery Stars. The Transformations of Native American Fiction*, University of Pennsylvania Press, Philadelphia 1999.

Rowe W. C., *Buried Alive: the Native American Political Unconscious in the Fiction of Louise Erdrich*, "Postcolonial Studies", Vol. 7, No. 2, 2004, pp. 97-210.

Treuer D., *Native American Fiction – A User's Manual*, Graywolf Press, Minneapolis 2006.

Welch J., *Fools Crow*, Penguin Books, New York 1986.

Welch J., *The Death of Jim Loney*, Penguin Books, New York 1979.

Welch J., *The Heartsong of Charging Elk*, Anchor Books, New York 2000.

Wilson J., *The Earth Shall Weep. A History of Native America*, Grove Press, New York 1998.

Zamora L. P., *Magical Romance/Magical Realism: Ghosts in U.S. and Latin American Fiction* [in:] *Magical Realism: Theory, History, Community*, L. P. Zamora, W. B. Faris (eds.), Duke University Press, Durham-London 1995.

KHALIL A. ARAB
MATEUSZ M. KŁAGISZ
ⓘ http://orcid.org 0000-0003-0807-3290

ON (SELF-)REPRESENTATIONS OF MASCULINITY IN SIYĀMAK HERAWI'S SHORT STORIES

Le mâle n'est mâle qu'en certains
instants, la femelle est femelle toute sa
vie, ou du moins toute sa jeunesse.[1]

Abstract: The article deals with masculinity in Afghan culture. Research data consist of five stories selected from the collection *Buy-e behi* (*The scent of quince*) by modern Afghan writer living in exile – Ahmad-Ziyā Siyāmak Herawi. The theoretical basis of the research are texts by Terry Eagleton and Pierre Bourdieu, supplemented by, *inter alia*, works of Élisabeth Badinter. The article consists of five parts. Part 0. presents the writer. Part 1. – methodology. Part 2. summarises five stories. Part 3. discusses (self-)representations of masculinity in Afghan culture. Part 4 is a summary.

Keywords: masculinity, Afghanistan, literature

0. ■

In our contribution to the project – *Manifestations of Male Energy in the World's Cultures* – we shall discuss literary (self-)representations of masculinity that can be found in a collection of short stories *Buy-e behi* (*The scent of quince*) by the contemporary Afghan writer Ahmad-Ziyā Siyāmak Herawi.

---

[1]   J. J. Rousseau, *Émile ou de l'éducation*, p. 190.

0.1. Our reason to start a discussion on (self-)representations of masculinity in modern Afghan literature is the increasing interest this topic has garnered during the past decade.[2] We would like our text to be a supplement to that discussion, because, as Shahin Gerami writes, studying so-called concepts of Muslim masculinities facilitates women-/gender-/men-oriented research in Islamic and general studies.[3]

0.2. Currently living in the United Kingdom, Siyāmak Herawi is a modern Afghan Dari-speaking novelist, writer, journalist and former diplomat.[4] Born in 1968 in a village near Herat, he moved with his parents to Kabul in 1980 where he enrolled at the prestigious high school Lise-ye Habibiya (Lycée Habibia). In 1984 he entered the Department of Persian Language and Literature at the capital university and soon afterwards received a scholarship to study Russian literature in Stavropol (today's Russia). He earned his MA degree defending his thesis on culture and history in Leo Tolstoy's works. Upon his return to Kabul in 1991, he worked as a journalist until 1996, while between 2002 and 2004 he served as the editor-in-chief of the all-Afghan newspaper *Ruznāme-ye Anis* (*Anis Newspaper*). In 2004 he was appointed deputy spokesperson for the president Hāmid Karzay (2001–2014), in 2013 as deputy spokesperson for the Ministry of Foreign Affairs. Between 2015–2017 he worked as the Chargé d'Affaires in the Afghan Embassy in London. His first book, *Morq-e toḥm-telāyi* (*The Golden Goose*, 1984, reprinted: 1985, 2000, 2017), is a collection of western Afghan popular folk tales that he compiled at the beginning of the 1980s. He believes the source of his inspiration was an illiterate old man called Kākā Rāhim (Uncle Rāhim) who was a great storyteller with incredible narrative skills. Being harassed by the Taliban regime (1996–2001), he decided to move to a secluded area in the countryside somewhere in the north-west of Herat. That time he used to accompany his close friend and other acquaintances whenever they went hunting. On these expeditions he developed a keen sense of observation, realising the close relationship between human and nature, determining the phenomenon of bioregionalism.[5] The knowledge of rural Afghanistan gained during that time re-appears in most of his

---

[2]   *Iran-namag.*
[3]   S. Gerami, *Islamist Masculinity and Muslim Masculinities*, p. 448.
[4]   All biographical information has been collected during personal conversations.
[5]   On bioregionalism see i.e.: S. Dant Ewert, *Bioregional Politics: The Case for Place*, pp. 439–451; D. Flores, *Place: An Argument for Bioregional History*, pp. 1–18; W. L. Lang, *Bioregionalism and the History of Place*, pp. 414–419.

works, especially in the *Gorghā-ye Dawander* (*Dawander's Wolves*, 2011), *Sarzamin-e Ǧamila* (*Ǧamila's Homeland*, 2012), *Tālān* (*Booty*, 2013) and *Bāzgašt-e Hābil* (*Return of Abel*, 2014). Such traces can also be found in his *Buy-e behi* – it is not a coincidence that most of his characters are village people.

1   ■

We have based our research on literature- and anthropology-oriented pillars. While the former is represented by Terry Eagleton's considerations on the nature of the character,[6] the latter is represented by Pierre Bourdieu's conceptions of masculine domination.[7]

1.1. Eagleton has firm opinions on the nature of characters as he suggests that "to show men and women as they really are is to show them as changeable, inconsistent and self-divided."[8] He additionally claims that characters have no pre- and post-history,[9] yet we are still able to conjure images of their personalities because in order to get the "essence" of individuals, i.e. to understand what makes them specifically themselves, we use generic terms.[10] This is, in our opinion, a crucial feature that brings literature and life closer to each other as well as providing a better insight into our topic. It is true that looking at Siyāmak Herawi's work through the prism of realist fiction, we can consider his characters – just like the characters of other realist writers – to be more defined/better realised when they are more individuated. But if they were not to some extent also types with traits/qualities we have previously encountered via literature sensu largo and/or socio-cultural relations, they would be incomprehensible. Such *déjà connu* qualities enable us to understand *pas encore connu* characters better. Eagleton also writes that there is no private life that has not been influenced by the wider public one, therefore a realist novel tends to grasp individual life in terms of histories, communities, kinship and institutions.[11] Characters are thus seen as being

---

[6] T. Eagleton, *How to Read Literature*, pp. 45–79.
[7] P. Bourdieu, *Masculine Domination*; idem, *Masculine Domination Revisited*, pp. 189–203.
[8] T. Eagleton, op. cit., p. 77.
[9] Ibidem, pp. 46ff.
[10] Ibidem, p. 55.
[11] Ibidem, 13, p. 64.

caught up in a web of complex mutual dependencies formed by social and historical forces; shaped by processes of which the characters may be only partially conscious.[12]

1.2. While Eagleton makes us think how individuals' "real/true" images appear in literature, Bourdieu forces us to ask: What makes individuals to be understood as "true/real" (self-) representatives of masculinity/femininity? For Bourdieu the core element of masculinity coalesces around the human body and, consequently, sexuality.[13] Nevertheless, he does not suggest that the hierarchical division of social roles and positions between men and women results from biology or erotic topography based on the top-bottom composition of their bodies in sexual intercourse. In his understanding, the composition itself is forced by socio-cultural ideas about intersexual relations transforming intercourse into a manifestation of male domination over a female partner, rather than making it a source of such supremacy. Consequently, anyone who violates the composition, like Sārā, one of Siyāmak Herawi's female characters, endangers the social order.[14] It is little wonder that a deeper analysis of Bourdieu's consideration shows that masculinity, being in fact a logical construct created in a unitary/collective mind, is not a mere transposition of the anatomic features of the human body into the framework of society even if "[t]he biological difference between the sexes (...) can (...) appear as the natural justification of the socially constructed difference between the genders, and in particular of the social division of labour."[15] Masculinity appears here as a mutable and modifiable phenomenon which undergoes constant negotiations in the context of, *inter alia*, femininity. Additionally, masculinity is not a native appearance but an adaptive one, since male individuals undergo masculinisation, i.e. become men, passing various short-/long-term *rite de passage*, for example separation from the mothers "to virilize them by stripping them of everything female which may remain in them."[16] For that reason it cannot be understood as something neutral and Bourdieu is right in claiming that only intergenerationally transmitted cultural codes of behaviour make masculinity unmarked. Its indeterminacy has

---

[12]   Ibidem, pp. 63–64.
[13]   P. Bourdieu, *Masculine Domination*, pp. 7ff.
[14]   Ibidem, pp. 19–21.
[15]   Ibidem, p. 11.
[16]   Ibidem, p. 27.

been detected by Michael S. Kimmel who writes that "(...) men are the »invisible« gender. Ubiquitous in positions of power everywhere, men are invisible to themselves."[17] Nevertheless, each culture holds within itself general ideas about what it means to be a man, and what rights and duties result from the fact of being a man.[18] Our goal is to look for such ideas, interwoven into the fabric of Siyāmak Herawi's selected short stories.

1.3. To analyse literary (self-)representations of masculinity, we need to use a tool that is a combination of both literary criticism represented by Eagleton and the anthropological approach represented by Bourdieu. Although John Orr writes that both, i.e. Bourdieu and Eagleton, "are worlds apart,"[19] socio-culturally created and intergenerationally transmitted patterns of masculinity leave (in)visible marks in the unitary (or collective) mind of the human and character, prompting us to link their approaches. As Eagleton emphasises, a psychoanalytic reading of the novel does not need to be an alternative to the sociological interpretation of it. "We are speaking rather of two sides or aspects of a single human situation."[20]

2.

The collection *Buy-e behi* consists of ten short stories. It was published in 1395 (2017) by Našr-e Zaryāb Publishing House in Kabul.

2.1. A common denominator of all the short stories is the socio-cultural question of male-female relations.

2.2. The language of the collection is, like all of Siyāmak Herawi's works, simple but far from naïve. The author thus makes his literature more accessible to Afghan readers representing all the multi-ethnic/-cultural society. This simplicity also brings him near to A'zam Rahnaward Zaryāb (1944–2020) who "according to Afghan readers is the only novelist writing in a literary and at the same time simple and clear style."[21] Nevertheless, he does not use exactly the same narrative techniques and

---

[17] M. S. Kimmel, *Invisible Masculinity*, p. 29.
[18] P. Bourdieu, *Masculine Domination*, pp. 25ff.
[19] J. Orr, *Hidden Agenda: Pierre Bourdieu and Terry Eagleton*, pp. 126.
[20] T. Eagleton, *Literary Theory. An Introduction*, p. 153.
[21] B. Bielkiewicz, *A'zam Rahnaward Zaryab. Koniokrad*, p. 173 – English translation M.M.K. and A.A.K.

he possesses an individual writing style that until recently was more au-
thor-oriented rather than reader-oriented. His reader-oriented approach
is reflected as understatement, leaving readers more room to further develop the store if they so want.

2.3. Generally, the third-person narrative is applied and only in two
cases does Siyāmak Herawi use the second-person perspective which is
unchartered territory in contemporary Afghan literature.[22]

2.4. We proceed our analyses with a brief plot summary of five stories: 1° *Sotwār-i ke dud šod* (*The sturdy man who turned into smoke*);
2° *Bud-o na-bud* (*To be and not to be*); 3° *Hesrat* (*Envy*); 4° *Del-i ke ris
ris šod* (*The heart that was shattered*); and 5° *Sāye-ye larzān* (*The trembling shadow*).

2.4.1. In the *Sotwār-i ke dud šod* a young man named Musā who dreams
of a pari (a supernatural female creature) is told that to find his beloved
he must go to the Ḥāğa Sarmaq shrine. People believe that its rooms are
full of paris that only the righteous can see. Overcome with joy, Musā
finds a group of men smoking hashish there. They explain to him that in
order to see his pari he needs to smoke and then to go to Ālenğān Creek.
Thenceforth Musā lives in the shrine for the next forty years, smoking
hashish and sitting frequently by the river talking with someone. One
winter's day he sees the pari. Trying to reach her hand, he falls into the
water and the strong waves sweep him away.

2.4.2. In the *Bud-o na-bud* the deaf and mute Sobhān has been a friend
with Sārā since childhood. One day her father informs his wife and
daughter that he wants Sārā to get married to Tālebče. During one of
her visits, Sobhān's mother – Zolayḫā – reveals to her son that Sārā is
to be forced into marriage. He is heartbroken while she storms out of
their house in a rage with his mother. It is only after that incident when
she is convinced that Sobhān is in love with her. Locking herself in her
room, she fantasises a happy future with Sobhān and Siyāh-Guš – their
favourite childhood dog. Her dream is shattered by a loud cry let out by
Zolayḫā who informs her of Sobhān's death.

2.4.3. In *Hesrat* Amir is an Afghan emigrant to Russia who has met
a local girl named Zinā (Russian: Зина). Although they live together for
some time, Amir announces unexpectedly his decision to go to Sweden.
In reply she informs him about her pregnancy. Amir leaves the country when his son – Rostam – is eight months old. Once in Sweden he is

---

[22]   K. A. Arab, *Negāh-i be Buy-e behi*, p. 7.

granted asylum. Forgetting about his Russian family, he starts a new life by marrying an Afghan girl, Sorayā, but the newly-wed bride divorces him after only a year. Amir thus seeks comfort in alcohol and prostitutes until he suffers a heart-attack. Following his recovery, he finds himself alone and decides to come back to Russia to look for Zinā and Rostam. When he is driven away by Zinā, his son comes after him and finds him sitting in a nearby park. Amir realises how both he and his son are identical. Rostam drinks his father's vodka, lights himself one of his cigarettes and asks if Amir has any money. Then he takes a few notes and walks away without speaking a word to Amir.

2.4.4. In the *Del-i ke ris ris šod*, Širin becomes suspicious of her husband – Ayyub – fearing that he might be having an affair. Three years after their marriage she sees that despite all his initial promises he has lost interest in her and their sex life has been reduced to almost non-existence. She does everything to please Ayyub but is unsuccessful. All her suspicions are confirmed when Aunt Qamar – an elderly woman living next door – comes to bake her bread in Širin's house. She admits that a rumour is circling around that Ayyub is planning to re-marry because Širin is infertile. Her heart sinks upon hearing this news and gives the dog a loaf of bread she had made for her husband.

2.4.5. In the *Sāye-ye larzān*, one night Amir is drawn by the sound of a flute that is being played in the far distance. He follows it into a shack where he is confronted by an old man who starts telling him a tale. Amir is terrified when he finds out that the old man knows about his love affair with Zahrā – the wife of Murād-ḫān, his overlord – as well as their plot to murder him. The old man explains to Amir that Zahrā does not really love him as she is really in love with Heydar – a rich and charismatic landowner – and is planning to marry him. She was simply using Amir to get rid of Murād-ḫān. As the music stops, Amir suddenly hears a voice authoritatively ordering him to play the flute. He turns his head, just to see Heydar standing on the doorstep with a rifle in his hand pointing at Amir.

3.

When examining the (self-)representations of masculinity in multi-ethnic/-linguistic Afghanistan, it is necessary to take into account two interrelated perspectives: 1° symbolic; and 2° social.[23] The symbolic (self-) representations of masculinity, were rooted, above all, in the locally understood *Qur'ān* and *sunnah*. The social / cultural aspect of masculinity and its (self-)representations, however, can be understood as a development stage in the lives of individuals, families as well as communities. These socio-cultural (self-)representations of masculinity can be reconstructed on data extracted from ethnographic documents, *inter alia*, songs, parables, local legends or classical / modern literature.[24] To learn about Siyāmak Herawi's male characters, we the readers need to listen not only to an omniscient narrator but also to the female protagonists, i.e. mothers, sisters, daughters, wives and / or female neighbours. By dint of the strategically limited information scattered around each story, we are able to re-construct wholly or partially (self-)representations of masculinity as each Siyāmak Herawi's male character, i.e.: 1° Musā, 2° Bābā, 3° Sobhān, 4° 'to', 5° Rostam, 6° Ayyub and 7° Amir manifest a unique form of masculine energy. Some of them still remain boys, some have successfully become men and finally some have not yet completely finished the process of masculinisation. Individualised masculinity appears hence as a mutable and modifiable socio-cultural phenomenon undergoing continual negotiation in the context of, *inter alia*, femininity.

3.1. Musā is the only one of Siyāmak Herawi's characters that can be observed from a double boy-man perspective. We meet him when he is about sixteen year old and is living with his parents somewhere in the countryside. Eagleton writes that: "[l]iterary figures have no pre-history,"[25] therefore, we are unable to comment on Musā's past. Indeed, we are unable to speak about the past of other characters of Siyāmak Herawi either, but we the readers do not need to have a prior understanding of their personalities. For us, Musā's identity comes into being at the beginning of the story, i.e. one cold winter's day when he meets a *pari*. She does not feel

---

[23]   See Sacha's research on gynephobia in the Hindu culture (M. Sacha, *Ginefobia w kulturze hinduskiej. Lęk przed kobietą w dyskursie antropologicznym i psychoanalitycznym*, p. 98).

[24]   There are various sources of socio-cultural codes of behaviour in non-monolithic Afghanistān that are ethnically/regionally limited, e.g. the *Paṣtunwali* among the Pashtuns and the *Mayār* among the Baluch people – both often contradict the Quranic rules and replace them if necessary (J. Pstrusińska, *Paštunwali – afgański kodeks postępowania*, pp. 63–79; L. Rzehak, *Doing Pashto. Pashtunwali as the ideal of honourable behaviour and tribal life among the Pashtuns*, pp. 1–21; W. Steul, *Paschtunwali. Ein Ehrenkodex und seine rechtilche Relevanz*). One should mention here also the unwritten codes of honour of the *kake* "youth, vagabond, warrior" (S. M. Talāš, *Ā'in-e kākagi*).

[25]   T. Eagleton, op.cit., p. 46.

deep shame in taking her clothes off and tantalisingly exposing her body; being of a supernatural nature, she is not limited by (socio-)culturally constructed and intergenerationally transmitted codes of behaviour. We, the readers, witness their sexual intercourse which is most likely Musā's first time. Although it is the *pari* who encourages Musā to play an active role, saying: "Ey Musā, kiss me! I belong to you, this body belongs to you, kiss me and infatuate me,"[26] one can ask who in reality is in charge. Bourdieu writes: "[i]f the sexual relation appears as a social relation of domination, this is because it is constructed through the fundamental principle of division between the active male and the passive female"[27] and continues: "(...) this principle creates, organizes, expresses and directs desire – male desire as the desire for possession, eroticized domination, and female desire as the desire for masculine domination, as eroticized subordination or even, in the limiting case, as the eroticized recognition of domination."[28] Their sexual intercourse is of great importance as in the eyes of Musā it is the first step towards manhood. The second one would be their marriage as the ceremony appears to be a turning point that proves a bridegroom is a "true/real" man. That is why he urgently wants to marry the *pari*. As Elisabeth Badinter writes, a man who wants to prove his masculinity, needs first of all to prove he is not a boy any more.[29] The problem is that he is still recognised by his parents as a child even if the *pari* calls him *širmard* "lionheart", *pahlawān* "champion" and *sotwār* "firm". The question of Musā's manhood becomes a topic of rather harsh discussion between him and his parents. In particular, his father looks at his son as a child, emphasising that a mere moustache or beard does not in itself make him a man. The prejudiced father appears here as a protector of the traditional family hierarchy, one who does not want to give up his place to his adolescent son. He does everything to humiliate him in front of his mother, like the time when Musā is not able to kill a fly. In an argument between the son and father, it is the mother who sides with Musā, but even for her he is only a boy – the Oedipus complex (?). Her undermining-his-manhood opinion makes him so angry that he directly says: "If I had a wife, you would have eight grandchildren by now."[30] Are his

---

[26]   A. Z. Siyāmak Herawi, *Bu-ye behi*, p. 70 – all English translation by M.M.K. and K.A.A.
[27]   P. Bourdieu, *Masculine Domination*, p. 21.
[28]   Ibidem.
[29]   E. Badinter, *XY: tożsamość mężczyzny*, p. 48.
[30]   A. Z. Siyāmak Herawi, op. cit., p. 76.

words somehow related to his initial sexual intercourse and awakening masculinity? Partially yes, but they also refer to the third step towards masculinity – the strong need to father a child. The mother's love towards Musā is so strong that she bows to his pressure and goes in search of the *pari*. Furthermore, she is not able to hide from him the truth that his beloved is in fact not a real girl but a supernatural being from an isolated place like the Ḥāǧa Sarmaq shrine. As Bourdieu writes "(...) the so-called rites of 'separation' (...) aim to emancipate the boy from his mother and to ensure his gradual masculinization by encouraging and preparing him to confront the external world."[31] It seems that in the case of Musā, such rites of "separation" are not carried out properly. His entry into the shrine should be understood as the beginning of his separation from the family. Neither his father, nor his mother are able to prepare their son to confront the world. In fact, it is this unpreparedness for relations with women that brings him misfortune.

3.2. There are two oppositional male characters in the *Bud-o na-bud*: 1° Bābā – Sārā's father, and 2° Sobhān – her neighbour and childhood friend.

3.2.1. Being almost absent, Bābā appears in the story only once and very briefly, but even so, he is the one who dramatically changes the tension of the narration. He is not the main character but is still the only one who plays the most crucial role in the lives of others; he is apparently the only one who is entitled to decide about their destinies. Bābā can be hence understood as the quintessence of masculinity – a husband and a father who simply informs his female relatives about his decisions without asking their opinions. We do not know on what basis, apparently visible anatomic changes, he comes to the conclusion that Sārā has become a woman and that it is time to marry Tālebče. Obviously, in traditional communities marriage is an agreement between two families rather than a free choice for a boy and a girl, but it is not only men who conform to this tradition, as women partake in the practice too. It is no wonder then that it is Sārā's mother who without sympathy explains to her: "Women have no choice. My mother did not. Nor did I, and neither will you, nor your daughters."[32] One can say that if men depersonalise women by depriving them of a voice, it is Bābā who makes his wife and young daughter mute with regard to Sārā's future. No-one expects him

[31] Ibidem.
[32] Ibidem, p. 23.

to explain about his decision because, as Bourdieu writes: "[t]he strength of the masculine order is seen in the fact that it dispenses with justification: the androcentric vision imposes itself as neutral and has no need to spell itself out in discourses aimed at legitimating it."[33]

3.2.2. If Bābā enters the stage and almost immediately exits it, Sobhān patiently waits in the wings to appear in front of the audience. He is the only one of Siyāmak Herawi's characters that got stuck in a liminal phrase between childhood and adulthood. The seriously ill, deaf and mute eighteen-year-old Sobhān lives together with his mother in a poor house. He is not a boy anymore but also not yet a man. As we know, characters have pre-history but probably Sobhān's world has become smaller recently because of his non-specified disease. It seems thus that his condition has a triple meaning. Literally, it is a serious and terminal health problem, different from deafness and muteness. Metaphorically, it should be understood as the inability to be masculinised – Sobhān has no father that would help him to become a man by completing a Bourdieu-esque rite of "separation" and a local mullah who could play the role of a guide here is not interested in carrying out such a task. Symbolically, it should be understood as a visible symptom of being in love with Sārā. Sobhān is, to some extent, the opposite of Bābā. While for Bābā she is only the third girl, for Sobhān she is the first and only one in his life, with the exception of the mother of course. Being deaf and mute, he is still able to express his feelings towards Sārā when he follows her body – her mouth, hair and finally breasts – with his eyes. Or when he (un)consciously chews her finger while consuming a cucumber – a single bite is not a childish mistake but rather a deliberate act. Ultimately, Sobhān's condition improves slightly when Sārā is next to him and we the readers can only guess that he is getting better whenever she takes care of him. Nourishing, a woman's obligation,[34] can bring the two sides, active and passive, i.e. someone who nourishes and someone who is nourished, closer to each other. Nourishing can also be of a sexual character to some extent, after all, the fruit that Siyāmak Herawi chooses, i.e. a cucumber, can be deemed erotic *per se*. Sobhān's construct of masculinity appears incomplete and fragile precisely because of being placed between childhood and adulthood. As Badinter writes,

---

[33]   P. Bourdieu, *Masculine Domination*, p. 9.
[34]   P. Bourdieu, *Le sens pratique*, p. 358.

a boy must be taken by someone from his mother to become a man.[35] The problem is that this person cannot be another woman. This is why the homo-erotic scene of consuming cucumbers, understood as one stage in the long-term process of Sobhān's masculinisation, is suddenly stopped by his mother, who, without regret, informs her son about Sārā's betrothal. Sobhān comprehends what has happened and that he will never be together with Sārā. For that reason, both resemble to some extent the famous lovers Laylā and Mağnun. The decision of Sārā's/Laylā's father to betroth his daughter against her will devastates Sobhān/Mağnun. But there are some differences between these two couples as it is Sārā, not Sobhān, who, starts dreaming about their life together, becoming a *mağnun* "a possessed, mad(wo)man." All of them are however caught up in an Eagletonian web of complex mutual dependencies formed by social forces and shaped by processes of which they are only partially conscious.[36] Interestingly, while Sārā imagines her life with Sobhān, he gets his voice back, and that makes her upset: "He says: »Yes, but instead I'm not deaf and mute anymore, I can speak.« You say: »No, I don't like this exchange. I want my deaf and mute Sobhān«."[37] She rejects voiced Sobhān, but why? Apparently, she knows that if Sobhān could speak, he would only deprive her of her own ability to speak, masculinity and femininity vying with each other for total control.

3.3. There are two male characters in the *Hesrat*. The narrator who calls himself "to (you (sg.), thou)" and his son named Rostam.

3.3.1. The main character of the *Hesrat* is SH's only male character who speaks for himself. We meet him when he is considering whether to knock on the door of a long-lost cohabitant named Zinā or not. His growing anxiety regarding her reaction contrasts with his determination to abandon her and their newly-born son sixteen years earlier. He expresses deep sorrow and repentance, but as one reads on more carefully, one can wonder if his return to Moscow is caused by true remorse or it is merely cold calculation. Ultimately, he had no objections to inform her one winter's day that he was moving to Sweden to apply for asylum. Admittedly, he assured her that he would bring her, but we cannot be sure if that was really genuine. Time showed that he did not intend to keep his word. Soon after leaving Moscow, he forgot about his family and

---

[35]   E. Badinter, op. cit., p. 75.
[36]   T. Eagleton, op.cit., p. 64.
[37]   A. Z. Siyāmak Herawi, op. cit., p. 45.

decided to start a new life. Furthermore, his reasons for emigrating, i.e. unspecified problems with the local police and mafia, seem to have been just a pretext to leave Russia and to break with Zinā. As he explained himself, what was supposed to be just a passing romance turned into an unintended relationship, even if it was the narrator who first said "I love you."[38] We have an opportunity to watch him over breakfast, when, as if nothing had happened, he tells her about his decision. He does not respond to her despair and quietly finishes his omelette and tea, but the look on his face changes suddenly on hearing the news of her pregnancy. He nervously begins to consider the various options on how to solve this problem. In his inner monologues, he throws worse insults at Zinā, calling her e.g. a permissive slut, a whore who became pregnant without marriage. The narrator believes naïvely that if Zinā could sleep with him without any formal registration of their relationship, she would sleep with other men too. He finally suggests that she have an abortion, saying that he never wanted a child. In fact, it is her problem, not his, and his proposal is simply a friendly favour. Although Zinā refuses to have an abortion, eventually giving birth to a son whom the narrator gives the name Rostam, it does not change his approach to the whole situation – the son, just like Zinā herself, must be thus considered a trap that the narrator needs to escape. After arriving in Sweden, he quickly decides to marry an Afghan girl which, as he emphasises, must be a virgin(sic!) – this term comes from Bourdieu's suggestion that "[m]anliness, virility, in its ethical aspect, i.e. as the essence of the *vir, virtus*, (…) remains indissociable, tacitly at least, from physical virility, in particular through the attestations of sexual potency – the deflowering of the bride (…)."[39] This time, the table turns and it is a newly married wife who, accusing the narrator of old-fashionedness and mismatching, wants to divorce him. The narrator, in a fit of rage, beats Sorayā who eventually ends their relationship. We can thus witness the gradual fall of the main character. Alcohol and cigarettes destroy his health. He has a heart attack and must be operated on. Simultaneously, we are witnessing the objectification of women as the narrator uses prostitutes – women changed from partners into objects of sexual possession only. Lonely, one day he remembers that he has a family in Russia. He explains that it would be good if someone could give him some tea in his old age, in other words,

[38]   Ibidem, p. 106.
[39]   P. Bourdieu, *Masculine Domination*, p. 12.

to serve him. His return to Moscow is thus understood as not an act of remorse but of calculation, with further objectification of the former co-habitant. Just like the narrator himself symbolically spat in Zinā's face, leaving her alone with the small child, it is she who now literally spits in his face. As one can see, there is no chance of reconciliation here and the *Hesrat* is an excellent example of Bourdieu-esque male domination that not only harms women's existence but also devastates men's personalities. The scene in which the narrator gives his son some money is of strong symbolic meaning. Disappointed by Rostam's attitude, lack of interest, terrified by his physical and mental state and horrified by the idea that his son has become an addict, the narrator looks dispassionately at the notes that the wind is blowing away from his hand and scattering across the street. He comes across as a rather affluent man with enough money to make Zinā's and Rostam's life better, but he already knows that it is impossible to repent for his sins and get back the time that he lost on his own accord.

3.3.2. The narrator claims that Rostam is his faithful copy in appearance. However, the problem is that it is a defective one, as Rostam, addicted to alcohol and cigarettes, wonders aimlessly around the city. What is more, Rostam also represents the complete failure of his namesake to be found in the *Šāhnāme* (*The Book of Kings*) by Ferdousi (10th/11th c.). Ferdousi's Rostam is the mightiest of Iranian heroes, who, as a child, slays the white elephant and tames the legendary stallion Raxš; as an adult he carries out a series of acts called *haft ḫān-e-Rostam* (the seven labours of Rostam) comparable to the Twelve Labours of Heracles. Since characters have no pre-/post-history, we can only speculate, but the fragile personality of Siyāmak Herawi's Rostam and the emotional problems that he tries to solve in the simplest and most destructive way, may have been shaped by the fact that his father abandoned him sixteen years before. As Badinter writes, it is a man that creates the man.[40] The problem arises when a proper mentor is absent. Who would lead a boy into adulthood?

3.4. Ayyub, just like another one of Siyāmak Herawi's character – Bābā – should be considered an invisible actor. We know more about him thanks to his wife – Širin. They wedded three years earlier and during that time he adored her very much, promising a lot, but their marital idyll did not last forever. Ayyub started changing, becoming moodier, curt and even violent. A story about an over-cooked meal reveals his

---

[40] E. Badinter, op. cit., pp. 73ff.

truculence towards Širin. Becoming upset, he breaks the pot into pieces and hits her quite hard. One may ask, why does he do that? There are two reasons that might explain his reaction. Firstly, Širin, in his opinion, does not meet the requirements of a wife; Bourdieu precisely divides various the activities between men and women and cooking is seen as a female obligation, one that she has failed to fulfil.[41] Secondly, and more importantly, she does not meet the requirements of a would-be mother, lest we forget about the bright future he was planning for their children. Ayyub expected Širin to bear him a child, a son, or at least a daughter, but instead he has no offspring yet. This is the main, and probably only reason why they started drifting apart rapidly. The quarrel over the meal hence shows his frustration and disappointment in how she has failed him as a wife. In his own eyes, and in the eyes of others he is not a man, or better to say, he has failed to prove once again that he is a man. As Bourdieu emphasises, if the number of children determines the social position of a woman, it also attests to the social value of a man.[42] Širin does everything to regain her husband's interest, so one day she cooks the best meal, waits carefully at the table, brings some tea, and when they are lying together in bed, it is she who tries to initiate sexual intercourse in the absence of his reaction; here one can speak of a reversal of the classic male-female role and it causes a sharp reaction from Ayyub. He interrupts her, leaving her surprised and ashamed in the bedroom alone. Ayyub has to react to her behaviour in such a harsh way because it is Širin who tries to usurp the active role reserved for him. No husband can allow his wife to take control over him during sexual intercourse as it would suggest that she controls him in a real life too. Eventually, though, they will have sexual intercourse but Širin still doubts the sincerity of his feelings. When Ayyub comes home dressed nicely one day, Širin is unaware, but he has made secretly some decisions regarding his, or better to say, their life together. He wants to take a second wife because the first one will never bear him children; his unexpressed presumption is of great significance here as he would never consider himself to be infertile because infertility is never a men's problem but only a women's fault. Ayyub behaves like Bābā, who, being disappointed at having yet another daughter, decides to marry another woman to have a son. The fact that his first wife speaks about other co-wives could suggest that

41 P. Bourdieu, *Le sens pratique*, p. 358.
42 Idem, *Masculine Domination*, p. 12.

even the second one has failed to fulfil his expectations. Polygamy is not just a problem for women. In fact, it is also a socio-cultural phenomenon that can harm both partners, even if men do not see it or do not want to see it. What is important here is the fact that Ayyub does not talk about his expectations with Širin, he does not treat her as a partner any more. His previous promises can thus be understood as manifestations of a Bourdieu-esque male desire to control women, but one can ask here whether there are any socio-cultural patterns that Ayyub would/could follow to establish a healthy relationship with Širin? – lest we forget about Sārā's mother's words. Instead, he forces her to accept his decision, informing her about it in the most painful and unpleasant way, through the agency of one of the biggest gossips in the village – Aunt Qamar. Why does Aunt Qamar decide to come to Širin's house to bake her bread? Why does, what seems to be a simple conversation at the beginning, turn into a bitter gossiping episode about Ayyub that eventually shatters Širin's dream? Is her only task to inform Širin about her husband's decision? In this short story, it is not only Širin who appears to be entangled in an Eagletonian web of socio-cultural dependencies. It is also Ayyub who cannot extract himself from them as they force him to have an offspring. Just like the time he proved he was a man by marrying Širin, he must show once again that he is a man by fathering a child. Without this crucial element, the socio-cultural construct of his masculinity will remain incomplete.

3.5. Amir – the main character of the final story – to some extent resembles Musā, both heroes are young and inexperienced. We watch them while they are becoming men, or, better to say, struggling to become men. One night Amir is suddenly awoken by the sound of a ney (flute) melody. Heading towards its source, he enters an old ruined shack in a cemetery and meets there an old grey-headed man playing the instrument. The shack changes consequently into his grave while the old man turns out to actually be his alter ego. As the stranger invites Amir to sit next to him and listen to a story, one can look at the beginning through the prism of the *Masnavi-ye ma'navi* by Moulānā (13th c.): "Be-šnou az ney (...)."[43] Moulānā speaks about two separated lovers, whereas Siyāmak Herawi about killing for love. Amir – a hired man working in Morād-ḫān's field – falls in love with his wife, Zahrā, and after some time allows her to persuade him to murder her husband. Amir kills Morād-ḫān,

[43]   Ǧ. M. M. Moulana, *Masnavi-ye ma'navi*, p. 21.

believing himself to be bold and clever but the stranger easily shows him to be rather craven and naïve. Amir thinks that Zahrā is in love with him, while, the stranger explains that she loves Heydar and has merely used him for her own purposes – just like her husband hired him to carry out work in the field, she hired him to carry out her plot. Bourdieu writes that sexual relations appear "as a social relation of domination,"[44] but here sexuality seems to be rather a tool of female supremacy, as it is Zahrā who encourages Amir to make love to her. She uses her body to take control of Amir but does that mean that she makes him a man? No, firstly because it is men who make men. Secondly because she is annoyed with him trembling when they lie in bed together, she resembles more his mother than his lover. Amir is unable to demonstrate Badinter's words that a man when wants to prove his masculinity needs first of all to prove he is not a boy any more.[45] The fact that Amir has not become a man yet, becomes clear in the murder scene. Killing someone is a masculine task, not a female one,[46] hence it is Zahrā who pushes Amir towards the murder. But the act itself must be done properly. Instead, Amir kills Morād-ḫān by cowardly stabbing him in the back, literally and figuratively. What is interesting, after murdering Morād-ḫān, with whom Amir was apparently friends, his personality starts to fragment. This fragmentation is clearly visible in the case of his emotionality that is represented by his own shadow. Amir pretends to be steady or calm but his shadow trembles and once even separates from the body for an instant – such separation indicates mental breakdown.

4.

What makes the characters of Siyāmak Herawi a true embodiment of ordinary Afghan men and women?[47] As Eagleton writes: "[t]he truth (...) is that human beings are uncommon only up to a point. There are no qualities that are peculiar to one person alone."[48] The characters share

---

[44]   P. Bourdieu, *Masculine Domination*, p. 21.
[45]   E. Badinter, op. cit., p. 48.
[46]   P. Bourdieu, *Masculine Domination*, p. 52.
[47]   K. A. Arab, op. cit., p. 7.
[48]   T. Eagleton, op.cit., p. 54.

hence some common features with us, the readers, and that makes them more realistic, not to say, "real/true." Siyāmak Herawi's characters found in the *Buy-e Behi* share some common features as well. Musā, Bābā, Sobhān, "to", Rostam, Ayyub and Amir control or try to take control of their female counterparts – a tendency that Bourdieu calls "masculine domination" and understands as a basic factor of male–female relations. Bourdieu-esque masculine domination appears in Bābā's, Ayyub's and "to"'s lack of interest in discussing their decisions with those whom they mostly concern. The Bourdieu-esque rite of "separation" appears in Musā's or Amir's problematic process of masculinisation and their inability to dominate female partners. All of them are trapped in the afore-mentioned web of complex mutual socio-cultural dependencies, e.g. Širin, who suspects her husband is influenced by spells cast by another woman. How is it even possible that a strong man can be manipulated by a weak woman? Is not a real man strong enough to overcome this? Or maybe on the contrary, he is of such a delicate and fragile nature that a woman can easily crush him if she really wants to. It reminds us of the *pari* who cast a spell on Musā leading him astray, as well as Zahrā who calls down death upon Amir. Siyāmak Herawi shows how complicated masculinity can be, for masculinity is not a native feature but an adaptive one since individuals undergo masculinisation and that masculinisation itself is a difficult, tough van Gennep-esque rite of passage. Some of his characters fail to become men, some can be called true male beings, but all of them are constructed in comparison to femininity, or better to say, both socio-cultural constructs are developed simultaneously and complementary.

BIBLIOGRAPHY

Arab K. A., *Negāh-i be Buy-e behi*, "Hašt-e sobh", 22 February 2017, p. 7.
Badinter E., *XY: tożsamość mężczyzny*, Wydawnictwo W.A.B., Warszawa 1993.
Bielkiewicz B., *A'zam Rahnaward Zaryab. Koniokrad*, "Przegląd Orientalistyczny", Vol. 3–4, Nos. 123–124, 1982, pp. 173–181.
Bourdieu P., *Le sens pratique*, Editions de Minuite, Paris 1980.
Bourdieu P., *Masculine Domination*, Stanford University Press, Palo Alto 2001.
Bourdieu P., *Masculine Domination Revisited*, "Berkeley Journal of Sociology", Vol. 41, 1997, pp. 189–203.
Dant Ewert S., *Bioregional Politics: The Case for Place*, "Oregon Historical Quarterly", Vol. 103, No. 4, 2002, pp. 439–451.
Eagleton T., *How to Read Literature*, Yale University Press, New Haven-London 2013.

Eagleton T., *Literary Theory. An Introduction*, John Wiley & Sons, Minneapolis 2003.

Flores D., *Place: An Argument for Bioregional History*, "Environmental History Review," Vol. 18, No. 4, 1994, pp. 1–18.

Gerami S., *Islamist Masculinity and Muslim Masculinities*, [in:] *Handbook of Studies on Men and Masculinities*, M. Kimmel, J. Heart, R. W. Connell (eds.), Sage, Thousand Oaks-London 2005, p. 448–57.

Iran-namag, "A Bilingual Quarterly of Iranian Studies", Vol. 3, No. 1, Spring 2018, Special Issue on Iranian Masculinities.

Kimmel M. S., *Invisible Masculinity*, "Society" 1993, Vol. 30, No. 6, pp. 28–35.

Lang W. L., *Bioregionalism and the History of Place*, "Oregon Historical Quarterly", Vol. 103, No. 4, 2002, pp. 414–419.

Moulana Ğ. M. M., *Masnavi-ye ma'navi*, Entešārāt-e Hemres, Tehrān 1382AP (2003-2004).

Orr J., Hidden Agenda: *Pierre Bourdieu and Terry Eagleton*, [in:] *Reading Bourdieu on Society and Culture*, B. Fowler (ed.), Blackwell Publishers, Oxford–Malden 2000, pp. 126–141.

Pstrusińska J., *Paštunwali – afgański kodeks postępowania*, "Etnografia Polska", Vol. 21, No. 2, 1977, pp. 63–79.

Rousseau J. J., *Émile ou de l'éducation*, Vol. II, Nelson Éditeurs, Paris 1914.

Rzehak L., *Doing Pashto. Pashtunwali as the ideal of honourable behaviour and tribal life among the Pashtuns*, "Afghanistan Analysts Network. Thematic Report", No. 1, 2011, pp. 1–21.

Sacha M., *Ginefobia w kulturze hinduskiej. Lęk przed kobietą w dyskursie antropologicznym i psychoanalitycznym*, Wydawnictwo Uniwersytetu Jagiellońskiego, Kraków 2011.

Siyāmak Herawi A.-Z., *Buy-e behi*, Kābol 1395AP (2016).

Steul W., *Paschtunwali. Ein Ehrenkodex und seine rechtilche Relevanz*, Steiner, Wiesbaden 1981.

Talāš S. M., *Ā'in-e kākagi*, s.n., Eslāmābād 1381AP (2002-2003).

KWASU DAVID TEMBO

POWER, MASCULINITY, AND WAR: SUPERMAN, A CASE STUDY

Abstract: To anyone with even a cursory knowledge of DC Comics' character, Superman can be regarded as a particularly notable example of a modern hero, an archon of moral probity and ethical altruism, and, despite being an alien from the planet Krypton, a symbol of physical masculine indomitability. As such, Superman is an ideal target for a deeper postmodern critique of the superhero as a reconstruction of the masculine aesthetic-narrative. Referring to Christopher Knowles' *Our Gods Wear Spandex: The Secret History of Comic Book Heroes* (2007), Larry Tye's *Superman: A High-Flying History of America's Most Enduring Hero* (2012), and Glen Weldon's *Superman: The Unauthorized Biography* (2013), this paper will discuss how the diegetic disruptiveness of the figure of Superman, that is, a set of his properties or features that include power (here understood as a manifestation of male or at least masculinised energy), and Otherness were institutionalised during the period of World War II. I will stress that it was at this point in the character's history that Superman became the moral and nationalistic icon it is still widely regarded as today: the point where the so-called "Man of Tomorrow" became the "Man of Steel." In doing so, this paper will perform an aesthetic and socio-historical close reading of the character to simultaneously theorise and historicise how Superman can be read as a marker of the socio-cultural value of masculinity in pre- and post-World War II America.

Keywords: power, masculinity, Otherness, World War II, Superman

INTRODUCTION

The topic of Superman and war has been described in multiple works, from multiple perspectives, across multiple epochs. These include works by the following: J. A. Mangan in his two edited texts *Superman Supreme: Fascist Body as Political Icon – Global Fascism* (1999) and *Shaping* the *Superman: Fascist Body as Political Icon – Aryan Fascism* (1999); Joseph J. Darowski's 2012 edited collection *The Ages of Superman: Essays on the Man of Steel in Changing Times*, which examines Superman's patriotism during World War II and his increase in power in the years of the Cold War; Mike Conroy's exploration of the graphic aspects of the relationship between comics and the war years in his 2009 *War Comics: A Graphic History;* and Cord Scott's 2007 article "Written in Red, White, and Blue: a Comparison of Comic Book Propaganda from World War II and September 11." In *Comic Book Nation. The Transformation of Youth Culture in America* (2003), Bradford Wright provides an edifying description of the socio-economic, sociopolitical, and cultural milieu of wartime America,

> (…) the war years were a boom time for most American industries, and the comic book industry was no exception. As defence spending finally pulled the nation out of the Great Depression, millions found work and brought home larger paychecks. Many workers had never had it so good, and neither had their children. More disposable income for Mom and Dad meant more nickels and dimes for kids to spend on comic books. In early 1942 *Publishers Weekly* and *Business Week* both reported that some 15 million comic books were sold each month.
> Moreover, publishers assumed generous "pass-along-value" of five readers per comic. By December 1943, monthly comic book sales had climbed to 25 million copies. As many as 125 different titles could be found at newstands every month. Retail sales of comic books in 1943 added up to nearly $30 million.[1]

In *Superman and the War Years: The Battle of Europe Within the Pages of Superman Comic,*[2] Wallace Harrington offers a more personal perspective of this milieu, imagining that "on some warm summer night in 1941, there must have been a couple of kids sitting on a hill overlooking a small town in Kansas who stared out at the stars and dreamed, 'If Superman were real he'd show those Nazis what for.' They would have dreamed, like every other kid who tucked a bath towel into their t-shirts and pretended to fly around the room, that Superman WAS real.

---

[1]   B. W. Wright, *Comic Book Nation. The Transformation of Youth Culture in America*, p. 31.
[2]   W. Harrington, *Superman and the War Years: The Battle of Europe Within the Pages of Superman Comics* [www 02].

And that if he somehow appeared and stood before them, right then, he would most definitely do the right thing because he was Superman. For he could 'change the course of mighty rivers and bend steel bars in his bare hands', and then, as now, Superman was the symbol of truth, justice and the American way."[3] In *War, Politics and Superheroes: Ethics and Propaganda in Comics and Film* (2011), Marc Di Paolo draws attention to Superman within the above described milieu and notes some very interesting paradoxes concerning the character and war that will be discussed in more detail below. For example, Di Paolo notes that "the end of World War II had robbed [the producers of the *Adventures of Superman* radio serial] of ripped-from-the-headlines opponents for Superman to combat, other than less-than-frightening Neo-Nazis and gangsters."[4] Di Paolo also goes on to propose that

(...) a popular misconception about Superman is that he is obsolete because he represents quaint, establishment ideas [and that] another complaint heard about Superman is that he is a God-like figure, too powerful for anyone to relate to. However, there are legions of far more reactionary superheroes – and far more all-powerful ones – who remain astonishingly popular with a right-leaning fan base. After all, what superhero is more invulnerable, more politically retrograde, and more beloved than The Punisher? Superman at least has Kryptonite as a weakness. The Punisher is a one-man army and cannot be killed. So the truth must lie elsewhere. In actuality, Superman represents a form of patriotic, transcendentalist liberalism that has fallen out of favour since the Reagan Revolution's repudiation of the politics of the New Deal and the eroding of Lyndon Johnson's Great Society. Liberals since the 1970s have lost their faith that their movement will ever gain momentum again, and that lack of faith undermines their patriotism and their interest in the Utopian hope for a better future that Superman represents. Conservatives, for their part, pay lip service to liking Superman because his costume is made from the colours of the American flag, but they secretly suspect that that he represents liberal ideas.[5]

[3]   Ibidem.
[4]   M. Di Paolo, *War, Politics and Superheroes: Ethics and Propaganda in Comics and Film*, p. 138.
[5]   Ibidem, p. 139.

In the DC Comics hyperdiegesis, Superman has come to represents many things to many people. Most conventionally, Superman is regarded as an archon of good will, altruism, and hope. However, this iconographic status as comic books greatest humanitarian was subject to a developmental arc spanning several decades of the twentieth century before becoming more or less fixed within the frameworks of both global popular culture and visual culture as well. The origins of Superman as an alien being with uncanny physical and behavioral similarities to a male human being, combined with the character's truculent sense of moral probity, a puerile ethical adroitness, and simplistic view of fairness, combines with the character's supra-human physical abilities makes Superman an interesting and complex figure of physical masculine power. Referring to Christopher Knowles' *Our Gods Wear Spandex: The Secret History of Comic Book Heroes* (2007), Larry Tye's *Superman: A High-Flying History of America's Most Enduring Hero* (2012), and Glen Weldon's *Superman: The Unauthorized Biography* (2013), this paper will analyze Superman, as both a representation of a modern superhero, and the changing values presented by him in pre- and post-World War II America in the context of the power understood as masculinized energy. In order to do so, this analysis will be divided into three sections predicated on specific historical periods of the character's diegetic and extradiegetic histories; that is: 1) pre-war, 2) during the war and, 3) after the war periods of time.

1. THE GOLDEN AGE (1930–1950): SUPERMAN, WAR, AND VIOLENCE

The issue of male or masculine energy in the Superman mythos truly begins during the period of World War II. A prefatory remark should be made here regarding the use of the term "male" or "masculine" to refer to Superman. Within the character's diegetic history, Superman is an uncannily anthropic alien being that expresses many seemingly identical superficial or physical traits as a human male. However, Superman is from the planet Krypton and is, onto-existentially speaking, essentially Other. This fact does not preclude the character from both identifying as well as living as male, thereby subscribing to the entire history of the sociopolitical, economic, and cultural issues and debates such an identity necessarily entails. The tensions latent within the relationship between power, Otherness, and the masculine body come to a global crisis both on and off the page during World War II. The Japanese attacked Pearl Harbor while *Superman*, Vol. 1, No. 13 (November, 1941) was on the stands. Pearl Harbor drew the United States into a war that would irrevocably alter the way the nation viewed both itself and its place in the world. Superman would also necessarily come to change with it because while the character had begun as the adolescent power fantasy of two awkward, emasculated boys, creators Jerry Siegel and Joe Shuster, who longed for something more than physical and socio-economic powerlessness, Superman would grow into the power fantasy of an entire nation at war. However, the character's vast powers became an editorial problem when America joined the war in December 1941. Readers, whose imaginations melded both on and off-page realities, could not help but think that if allowed, Superman would win the war swiftly and unaided.

Figure 1. Taken from *Look* magazine "How Superman Would End the War" (February, 1940). Written by Jerry Siegel, illustrated by Joe Shuster

After seeing Superman single-handedly reform an arms dealer and make peace with two warring factions of San Monte (which was an analogue for the ongoing Spanish Civil War at the time) in the first two issues of *Action Comics*, the necessity of Superman's active involvement in the war effort would seem self-evident. It was clear by the time America joined the war that Superman was a destructive creature, an organic doomsday device if weaponised and unleashed. This problem was further underscored in the 27 February 1940 issue of *Look* magazine (see Figure 1 above). In "How Superman Would End the War" written by Siegel and illustrated by Shuster, one witnesses the fury of a Kryptonian in pitched battle. Superman twists Nazi cannons into knots of scrap metal, intercepts Japanese fighter planes, and even captures Hitler and Stalin, presenting the two dictators before the League of Nations for judgement.

While this non-canonical story of how Superman would end the war was published before America had officially entered the war, once America joined the conflict in earnest, Superman altogether stepped back from active soldiering. In contrast, other notable patriotic role models filled page and screen with rallying calls to arms all around the character. Examples included: Ace of the Airwaves Hop Harrigan, ace pilot Blackhawk, who swore revenge against the Nazis after being shot down in 1939, Rip Carter and the Boy Commandos, Captain America, Captain Marvel, the Sub-Mariner, and the Human Torch. Despite this brigade of super-servicemen, Superman was sitting out the war. Young letter writers and editors of *The Washington Post* and *Time* magazine asked why this was the case. With "How Superman Would End the War," Siegel, Shuster, and DC editors Harry Donenfeld, and Jack Liebowitz knew they had created an expectation for their superpowered and morally righteous hero to intervene on behalf of the Allies. However, now the lives of U.S. soldiers were at risk and Superman could no longer be so cavalier about the horrors of war.

Unlike the character's comrades on the front, Superman was always and already operating at a different standard. Axis bullets did not bounce harmlessly off the chests of American soldiers and any story featuring a smirking Superman who could effortlessly destroy Nazi machine gun nests and mortar positions risked inappropriately trivialising the genuine trauma of the battlefield mortal soldiers experienced.[6] While the expectation of a non-superpowered individual, regardless of how heroic, may have been to harass, disrupt, and/or kill some of the enemy's troops, infrastructure, and supply lines, Superman's diegetic abilities created an extradiegetic expectation that it simply could not fulfil. Even an attempt

---

[6]   G. Weldon, *Superman: The Unauthorized Biography*, p. 54.

and failure of total victory would make Superman appear hollow, and therefore a liability to American troops' morale.[7]

This problem would come to be known as "Superman's Dilemma." The 13th April 1942 issue of *Time* described the problem as follows:

> Superman is now in a really tough spot that even he can't get out of. His patriotism is above reproach. As the mightiest, fightingest American, he ought to join up. But he just can't. In the combat services he would lick the Japs and Nazis in a wink, and the war isn't going to end that soon. On the other hand, he can't afford to lose the respect of millions by failing to do his bit or by letting the war drag on.[8]

The solution, often attributed to editor Murray Bolintoff and Shuster, was to have Superman officially, albeit ironically, declared unfit for battle. In a series of newspaper strips in 1942, Clark Kent tried to enlist in the Army. During an eye exam however, the character "accidentally" read a chart in the adjoining room with his X-Ray vision. While no other physical problems could be found with Clark, the Army doctor declared it 4-F, unwanted by the combat services of the United States military.[9] The solution succeeded, satisfying the entire spectrum of Superman readers from youthful comic enthusiasts, to the editors of *Time* magazine. In the same 1942 newspaper strip, Superman further distanced itself from the battlefront by declaring that the U.S. Navy, Marine Corps, Army, and Airforce was capable of overcoming their enemies without the intercession of his transcendent power, as if to suggest that the devastation of such a being's disruptive power and Otherness were simply beyond the purview of human warfare. Instead, Superman elected to dedicate his powers to the home front, battling saboteurs and fifth columnists who were thought to be attempting to destroy the production of war materials in America. In effect, Donenfeld and Liebowitz decided to turn the character into a symbol, an icon to boost morale, leaving the war effort to be fought and won by human soldiers who Superman referred to as "the greatest of all heroes, the American fighting man!"[10]

---

[7]   L. Tye, *Superman: A High-Flying History of America's Most Enduring Hero*, p. 58.
[8]   *The Press: Superman's Dilemma.*
[9]   L. Tye, op. cit., pp. 58–59.
[10] G. Weldon, op. cit., p. 54.

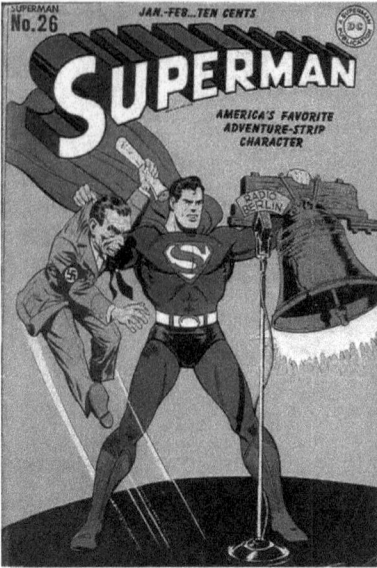

Figure 2. Taken from *Superman*, Vol. 1, No. 26 (January, 1944). Written by Bill Finger, illustrated by Ira Yarbrough

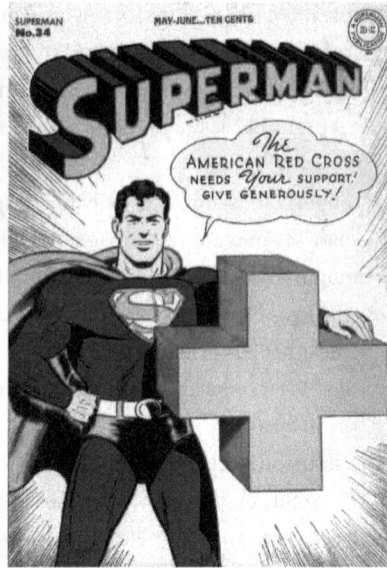

Figure 3. Taken from *Superman*, Vol. 1, No. 34 (May, 1945). Written by Don Cameron, illustrated by Sam Citron

Figure 4. Taken from *Action Comics*, Vol. 1, No. 76 (September, 1944). Illustrated by Ed Dobrotka

From this point onward until the end of World War II, Superman's direct confrontations with Hitler and Hirohito, or participation in the war effort more generally, were primarily confined to comic book covers. For example, Figure 3 shows Superman as a mascot of the Red Cross, while Figure 4 depicts Superman as an active combatant on the Pacific front. Similarly, Figure 2 shows Superman dangling Nazi propaganda minister Joseph Goebbels by the scruff of his neck while ringing the Liberty Bell, an iconic American symbol of independence, over the Berlin radio waves. Despite how attractive and attention-grabbing these covers were, they were largely, if not completely, unrelated to the content within. On them, U.S. servicemen and women were presented in conjunction with nationalistic and patriotic imagery and iconography to rally behind. In effect, Superman's cover artists produced propagandistic depictions of the character even before the United States entered the war. For example, on the cover of *Superman*, Vol. 1, No. 12 (September/October 1941), a beaming Superman proudly walks arm-in-arm with a U.S. soldier and seaman. However, once America entered the war, *Superman* and *Action Comics* cover artists were blatantly jingoistic with their aesthetic and iconographical treatment of Superman's power, body, and Otherness. For example, the cover of *Superman*, Vol. 1, No. 14 (January/February, 1942) shows Superman posing in front of a giant shield bearing stars and stripes, with an American eagle perched menacingly and majestically on his muscular forearm. Similarly, the cover of *Superman*, Vol. 1, No. 17 (July/August 1942) depicts Superman standing atop the Earth lifting Hitler and Hirohito by their necks in a pose that suggests that it is about to smash their skulls together. On the cover of *Superman*, Vol. 1, No. 18 (September/October 1942), Superman is shown astride a bomb as it descends on an unseen enemy position. Aside from the price, date, issue number, and the Superman title, the only other text printed on this cover reminds readers that "War savings Bonds and Stamps Do the Job on the Japanazis!", further emphasising both the character's martial efficacy and association with the American war effort. *Superman*, Vol. 1, No. 23 (July/August 1943) depicts one of the most famous wartime images of Superman. The perspective is from within a German U-Boat in which a pair of Nazi sailors look through a periscope. They see two things. The first, the boat they have just sunk. The second, Superman swimming toward them with a look of wrath on his face. The cover of *Superman*, Vol. 1, No. 24 (September/October, 1943) depicts Superman in his iconic pose, left arm akimbo, feet apart, chest out, proudly and heroically holding a billowing American flag. In the background, an idealised New York City sits peacefully at either dusk or dawn.

This jingoistic aesthetic also appeared on the covers of *Action Comics* from 1941 to 1945. Renowned Superman artists such as Wayne Boring, Joe Shuster, Fred Ray, and Jack Burnley consistently depicted Superman attacking Axis pill-boxes, destroying enemy tanks, or dismantling enemy submarines. The goal of the images on these covers was to conflate the character with the idea of the sociopolitical dominance of American ideology. This effect was achieved primarily aesthetically, by creating iconographic, geometrical, and symbolic (including colour) equivalence between Superman's cape and the American flag: between the red, yellow, and blue and the red, white, and blue. Donenfeld and Liebowitzs' cover artists were successful in this regard because the uniformity between Superman and Americanism took hold in the American consciousness. As a result, Superman was no longer seen as Other, no longer a Kryptonian seeking asylum on Earth, nor did the character's power or Otherness belong to himself any more. At the beginning of the war, Superman could have been accurately described an extremely popular children's character. However, by the time World War II had ended, Superman was regarded as *both* an American and a significant American icon. In this sense, the wartime history of Superman's mythos portrays him as an exemplar of successful cultural assimilation.[11]

Though Superman's jingoistic depictions featured extensively in *Superman* and *Action Comics* titles throughout the war, the fact that the most direct and patriotic depictions of Superman were ostensibly confined to the covers of the character's titles makes Superman's war effort appear somewhat peripheral or cosmetic. The covers bore little relation to the comics' content, making Superman's status as the greatest fighting American seem distant and exterior. Furthermore, in the months following the United States' official entry into the war, Superman stories took on a gradually, yet perceptibly, more whimsical and juvenile tone. While Superman's pre-war adventures featured spectacular feats in quotidian settings, the content of Superman's stories during the war came to include slapstick humour, bad puns, and increasingly bizarre plots. The character was no longer an active and dangerous socialist avenger. Instead, Superman's stories were now set in the realm of pure escapist

[11] Ibidem, pp. 55–60.

fantasy.[12] At that time, DC's newly instituted editorial board decreed that Superman was to no longer use his impressive physical power and energy to engage in acts of violence as he had before the war. As a result, Superman became less aggressive. Instead of unleashing his power in the pursuit of retributive justice, the character came to rely on his reputation and physical presence to dissuade criminals and evildoers where he had once employed terror and threats of physical violence to overcome them. During the war years, Superman had been de-clawed. The character's dangerous anti-establishment disruptiveness was turned into an institutional apparatus. No longer a "god-in-a-cape," a catalyst for new modes of being or subversiveness of any kind, or of socio-economic and existential turbulence, Superman became a placid entertainer.

In this sense, the war drastically changed Superman. Not in the way it did the character's on page/screen peers, like Steve Rogers (Captain America of Marvel Comics), who would return from the battlefields of the Pacific and European theatres of operation as combat veterans. Instead, during the war years, Superman encouraged readers to buy war bonds and save stamps, to plant Victory gardens, to give blood, and to collect scrap metal. Superman's patriotic image was cultivated *domestically* whereby the most powerful American comic book character up to and including the war years functioned as an auxiliary unit of national morale. By 1943, there was little to no trace of the vengeful and violent Superman of pre-war comics. This process of interpellation, here understood as Superman's self-recognition as an instrument of, the police and military State apparatuses, as well as American nationalist ideology,

> (...) smoothed Superman's rough edges and shaped him into something safer, more trustworthy. His social conscience morphed into boosterism. His sardonic smirk became a genial grin. Once hunted as a vigilante "mystery man," he now began working alongside the police. There was a war on, so the time for [socio-political reform] was over. Where once he agitated and chafed against the status quo, Superman was now determined to reinforce it.[13]

Superman and his colleagues served a very specific function during the war. They offered colourful diversions from the horrors and

[12] Ibidem, p. 60.
[13] Ibidem, p. 55.

difficulties of war, foreign and domestic, while simultaneously serving to distil American anxieties about the world's sociopolitical tumults by making them simple and assailable. The narratives of Superman, and character's like him, repeatedly reduced the complexities of global warfare to dialectical categories of good (the Allies), and evil (the Axis Powers). Whenever Batman, Superman, or Wonder Woman thwarted the fascistic machinations of the Axis powers and their acolytes, be they goons, scientists, or spies, the reader could engage in a reassuring war-by-proxy.

Ironically, at the same time, Superman's power, body, and Otherness were undergoing changes: the character was getting stronger. By *Superman*, Vol. 1, No. 16 (May/June, 1942), Superman went from being able to leap tall buildings in a single bound, to being able to fly through the stratosphere, hover in mid-air, and travel at light-speed. *Action Comics*, Vol. 1, No. 47 (April, 1942) depicts a Superman who had graduated from bending steel bars and smashing cars, to being able to tunnel through mountains with his fists alone. Superman's cognitive abilities increased as well and in *Action Comics*, Vol. 1, No. 62 (July, 1943), the reader learned that Superman possesses a "super-brain." The noteworthy significance of this increase here is that while the war years kept Superman's power, body, and Otherness in reserve in existential and revolutionary terms, instead of de-powering or maintaining the character's power-level, his strengths were paradoxically increased exponentially. Superman's power was something Donenfeld and Liebowitz needed to consume in acts other than warfare, yet it became more powerful in stasis, an accumulation or stockpiling of power, with no true challenge or channel within which to consume said power.

Superman's increased power directly reflected the nation's increasingly conflicted feelings about nuclear devices, their power, and who had access to them. However, the atomic threat was not reducible to a single extraterrestrial being because now human beings also possessed the power to destroy the world. For example, in *Action Comics*, Vol. 1, No. 101 (October, 1946), Superman is driven temporarily insane by an evil syndicate's secret chemical compound. As a result, Superman goes on a global rampage, destroying everything in his path until a nuclear test blast in the Pacific Ocean breaks the compounds' thrall. Similarly, in *Action Comics*, Vol. 1, No. 124 (September, 1948), Superman is made temporarily radioactive after being caught in a nuclear reactor explosion. This forces him to keep his distance from Metropolis, which in turn triggers a crime wave in his absence. Despite DC's whimsical mandate, these particular stories illustrate that Superman's creative teams still equated his powerful body with atomic power. Both were presented as incredibly powerful forces that had undeniably utopian and dystopian potentials.

1.1. TACTICAL POSTERITY

The decision to keep Superman in reserve during the war was one of Liebowitz's riskiest yet most profitable decisions. While the Boy Commandos and nearly all other comic book heroes who were combat veterans either faded in some way or disappeared entirely after the war, the reintegration into a peacetime society after the trauma of war was a problem for extradiegetic and diegetic soldiers alike. Figures like Hop Harrigan's popularity waned because they were supposed to provide an escape from the horrors of war. After the war however, their association with wartime America made them symbols of the realities of death, atrocity, and loss that the nation was trying to forget. DC's editorial board had made a successful decision in keeping Superman as an auxiliary instead of an active combatant that would come to pay large dividends. This decision of tactical posterity allowed Superman to change synchronously with the domestic market that would still be reading comics after the war concluded.

Both Superman as an icon and the nation the character represented went through a synchronous process of self-discovery during World War II. America learned that it had come to have a vibrant and malleable economy which it proved effective enough to forge a military industrial complex powerful enough to be instrumental in disabling the Axis war-machine. Similarly, Superman learned that it had grown stronger, able to defeat any enemy foreign or domestic. The stronger America became, the stronger Superman grew. The expansion of the American military industrial complex before and during the coming Space Race changed ideas concerning what the human race was, for better or worse, now capable of. The human race had grown from ballistic to nuclear, from mechanical and chemical to atomic. In response, Superman had to evolve to match the expanded public imagination, whose prevailing boundaries had literally been blown apart during World War II. In this sense, the increase of humanity's extradiegetic power needed be matched and superseded in the superbeing's diegetic representation of power. In this way, Superman's unison with the American public was fine-tuned during the war years.[14]

2. THE SILVER AGE (1950–1960): DISPLACEMENT OF MALE ENERGY IN POST-WAR AMERICA

I will now discuss the displacement of male energy as symbolised by the aesthetic and narrative handling of Superman's power during the 1950s to approximately 1970. This period was deeply influenced by the Atomic Age and the beginning of the Space Age. Superman and other comic book superbeings would come to represent the interests and lifestyle of a strong middle class, its fears and aspirations toward a clean, well-ordered, communitarian American society, and its assumptions concerning the idea of a centralised Federal government in a post-war America. The term communitarian here refers to the idea of a collection of interactions of a group of individuals, in a given geographical location, who share the same ideology, interests, and history. More specifically, communitarian ideals seek to support and increase the community's social institutions and social capital. With the emergence of the science heroes of the period, represented chiefly by characters like the re-imagined Flash and space-cop the Green Lantern in texts like *Showcase*, Vol. 1, No. 4 (October, 1956), and *Showcase*, Vol. 1, No. 22 (October, 1959), the science-heroes of the period notably championed a sociopolitical ethic that upheld a strong centralised government that represented a successful middle class. Differing from their counterparts of the 1940s, who championed a liberal Rooseveltian ideal by vilifying covetous corporate executives, "the new science heroes were proud servants of the military industrial complex."[15] While one could describe the heroes of the 1950s–1970s as obtuse, Knowles argues that they offered two things lacking in popular culture at the time namely, a positive and optimistic vision of society, while simultaneously providing heroes worth emulating.[16]

[14] L. Tye, op. cit., p. 64.
[15] C. Knowles, *Our Gods Wear Spandex: The Secret History of Comic Book Heroes*, p. 138.
[16] Ibidem.

In a sense, Superman was both most and least compatible with the ideals of the period. While Superman's power, as both boon and bane, spoke to the potentials and fears of the Atomic Age, Superman's Otherness spoke to the extraterrestrial aspirations of the Space Age. Despite this, the character's adventures in this period typically elected for a grounded, stifled, subservient, and domestic attitude toward his Otherness and a recalcitrant and nervous handling of his power and body, which reached a zenith in this period. Symbolically, Superman was much like a nuclear device in a nation's arsenal. With this deterrent in place and supreme power assured, instead of using that power to change the world, Superman often turned his power to bizarre and petty purposes in this period.

Many of Superman's adventures during the Silver Age dealt with "Imaginary Stories" in which both Superman's powers and the object of those powers were conveniently concluded so as to allow Superman to be completely domesticated. It should be noted here that it was a reaction to the book *Seduction of the Innocent*, in which psychiatrist Frederic Wertham blamed all comic books for society's ills and demoralization of youth and he labelled Superman a Nazi. DC and several other publishers had to save their image and created the Comics Code Authority (1954), which regulated comic books' content based on a strict set of guidelines, and everything: language, violence and sexuality were closely monitored. That is why DC introduced new shared universe (DC Universe) with alternate histories of characters. It consists of Earth-Two and Earth-One (the Golden Age versions of DC heroes resided on Earth-Two, while DC's Silver Age heroes were from Earth-One); that is why Superman, as the hero from the Golden Age continuity, married Louis Lane only on Earth-Two and it was one of alternative version of his life.

One particular trend in these Imaginary Stories saw numerous narratives that dealt with "the end of Superman's history" through the device of marriage, which also suggests that the measure of an ideal or utopian world in post-war America was reflected diegetically by diminishing the necessity for a superpowered hero of any kind. As such, I argue that from the 1940s to the 1950s, Superman's power, body, and Otherness all depreciate in order to conform to the post-war American ideal of a settled and lawful life. Additionally, I propose that this also led to a revaluation of the concept of the comic book superbeing from an icon of power and nationalist ideology, to a parodic and comical device. As Mark Cotta Vaz notes in *Tales of the Dark Knight* (1989), it is a

> (…) small wonder that by the time the war ended, many superheroes found it hard to go back to   busting bank robbers after the intensity of fighting the Axis aims of world conquest. The war in comic books despite its early promise, its compulsive flag waving, and its incessant admonitions to "keep 'em flying" was, in the end lost... from Superman on down, the old heroes gave up a lot of their edge.[17]

While the new science heroes of the period were proud servants of the military industrial complex, I also propose that some of the most bizarre and interesting Superman stories ever written come from Superman's post-war period. What I want to stress here is that the oddity of these narratives is a direct result of both writers and artists attempting to re-situate Superman's radically *physical* power, body, and Otherness in a *technologically* leaning, post-war society. While the character's powers had ironically increased during the years of a war he did not directly participate in, this battlefield absence also meant that it was not able to exhaust his accrued might in the conflicts of global warfare. I argue that such an excess of power resulted in excessive narratives that attempted to consciously mitigate or differ Superman's char, power, and Otherness.

2.1. DEFERRING POWER: WEISINGEREAN EXPANSION AND RETRACTION

Mort Weisinger's tenure as editor on Superman was marked by innovations that significantly disrupted the disruptiveness of the character's power, body, and Otherness. Innovations in terms of Superman's mythos, cast, and themes resulted in a diffusion of the value of these foundational aspects of the character through increasingly outlandish situations and plot devices. Under Weisinger's editorship, DC produced what were then new aspects of the Superman mythos that modern readers now regard as inextricable from the character itself. These included the creation of the Lois Lane and Jimmy Olsen spin-off titles *Superman's Girl Friend, Lois Lane* and *Superman's Pal, Jimmy Olsen, Supergirl,*

---

[17]   M. C. Vaz, *Tales of the Dark Knight*, p. 36.

Krypto the Super Dog, the Phantom Zone, the Bottle City of Kandor, the Legion of Super-Heroes, various explorations of the life, culture, and history of Krypton, and the various types of kryptonite.

With the invention of the Phantom Zone, Superman was no longer the Last Son of Krypton and had to share the miraculousness of his power and Otherness with both his cousin Kara Zor-El (Supergirl), and his new-found Kryptonian enemies, including Jax-Ur, General Zod, and later Faora Hu-Ul. Superman now also had a superpowered pet with the same powers as its master, including flight, physical invulnerability, and a human level intelligence. Furthermore, The Bottle City of Kandor allowed Superman to interact with other, albeit shrunken, Kryptonians, affording it opportunities to explore his history, people, and culture while still on Earth. Having access to Kandor, Old Krypton's capital city populated by thousands of Kryptonians, further diffused the character's sense of uniqueness, rendering his particular type of Kryptonian Otherness and power increasingly unremarkable. Moreover, the invention of kryptonite in *Adventure*, Vol. 1, No. 252 (September, 1958) not only made Superman mortally vulnerable, but devices like red kryptonite, with its unpredictable effects on Superman's behaviour, gave writers and artists a wide range of scenarios – humorous, thrilling, romantic, or melodramatic – to explore and develop Superman/Clark Kent as rounded characters. In Steven T. Seagle's meta-textual *It's a Bird...*,[18] Seagle describes the latent function of kryptonite as follows in the form of a mock-1950s advertisement:

> KRYPTONITE!!! Are you a VILLAIN trying to defeat the ULTIMATE man? Are you a WRITER trying to unlock the CORNER you've written yourself into by creating a SUPERMAN? A being so MIGHTY that the only way to DEFEAT him is to trump up a DEUX EX-MACHINA that can make a god UN-GODLY?!! KRYPTONITE! Takes the "Super" OUT of the "MAN."[19]

In accord with Seagle, I argue that the invention of kryptonite was ultimately intended to radically reduce or disrupt Superman's power, a power that was no longer necessary in such quantities after the war years. It was a device that made it easier for readers to relate to the

---

[18]   S. T. Seagle, T. H. Kristiansen, *It's A Bird...*
[19]   Ibidem, p. 37.

previously invulnerable superbeing. It is no coincidence that the period of the 1950s-1970s contains the most stories in which Superman loses his powers or has them significantly compromised in some way, leaving the character to not only save the day, but survive on his wits alone. Examples include "The Last Days of Superman" from *Superman*, No. 156 (1962) in which Superman erroneously believes that he has been infected by a rare Kryptonian virus. He thinks he is dying. Supergirl (Kara Zor-El, Superman's cousin and fellow surviving Kryptonian) manages to gather all of Superman's allies to tend to the requests on his last will and testament. This text shows that in the Silver Age, Superman's body, power, and Otherness can be completely stripped of any sense of danger or foreignness. It is as weak as we are. What godlike being of power needs to write a will? "The Showdown Between Luthor and Superman" from *Superman*, Vol. 1 No. 164 (1963) expands on the notion of a completely weak Superman by having Luthor and Superman fight on a planet where Superman's powers don't exist due to orbiting a red star. This text is part of a tradition in the Superman mythos that tries to humanise Lex Luthor and show that, without Superman, Lex may actually be a decent fellow. But more importantly, it is another example from the period of how the difficulty and disruptiveness of Superman's power, body, and Otherness is solved by totally reducing him to human being.

As such, during this period of innovation and creative expansion, Superman's power, body, and Otherness are consistently disrupted in two ways. First, directly, in the sense that the character is often exposed to a plot device which necessitates the temporary loss or disruption of the efficacy of his power, body, and Otherness. Second, the transformative or disruptive device bypasses Superman altogether and only affects Superman's supporting cast, therefore making Superman's power, body, and Otherness largely peripheral. Examples include Lana Lang receiving a ring in *Superboy*, Vol. 1, No. 10 (October, 1950) that enables her to transform various parts of her body into those of any insect. She designs a costume and calls herself "Insect Queen". It was Jimmy Olsen who underwent the most extreme and most frequent metamorphoses during the period, however. These include Olsen turning invisible (*Superman's Pal, Jimmy Olsen*, No. 40, October 1959), being transformed into a merman (*Superman's Pal, Jimmy Olsen*, No. 20 April 1957), developing a giant bald head to house his "super-brain" (*Superman's Pal, Jimmy Olsen*, No. 113 August/September

1968), and turning into a rampaging giant boy-turtle (*Superman's Pal, Jimmy Olsen*, No. 53, June 1961).

3. THE BRONZE AGE (1960–1970): DOMESTICITY, POWER, AND NOWHERE TO PUT IT

In order to widen the variety of stories that could be told, Weisinger invented the "Imaginary Story" line to explore non-canonical "what if?" scenarios that would otherwise be impossible under the rubric of the DC Multiverse's internal continuity and logic. The Imaginary Story also evidences an increasingly conspicuous trend toward matrimonial stability. For all Superman's canonical disinterestedness in Lois Lane in the 1940s, many Imaginary Stories of the 1950s-1970s examined the outcomes of Superman settling down and starting a family. These stories placed an ostensible premium on closure and happiness, symbolised by the binding union of marriage. This can be noted in the fact that the covers of many Superman stories during this period consistently depicted the character as a type of ultimate suburban father-figure, "The Amazing Story of Superman-Red and Superman-Blue!" by Leo Dorfman in *Superman*, No. 162 (July, 1963) being a particularly notable example (also see Fig. 7 and Fig 8 below). This particular narrative concludes with the two identical iterations of Superman, Superman-Red and Super-Blue, solving all the worlds sociopolitical problems, getting married, and living happily ever after. While the Imaginary Stories line was essentially an artistic space in which Superman's creative teams could explore even the most radical possibilities of the character's power, body, and Otherness with impunity, a series of Imaginary Stories that began in *Superman's Girl Friend Lois Lane*, Vol. 1, No. 19 (August, 1960) imagined the prescriptive and heteronormative married life of "Mr. and Mrs. Clark (Superman) Kent." These stories featured the couple dealing with domestic super-parenting in an idealised suburban paradise. What is important to note in this domestic turn in is that,

(…) when Superman's writers gave themselves licence to dream up anything they could, they invariably dreamed the American dream of the fifties, opting for the normative closure of marriage and family, of keeping house, cookouts, campouts, and, ultimately, a peaceful retirement. Most of Superman's

Imaginary Stories, whose very reason for being was to explore how radically the setup could get upset, ultimately offered their readers assurance that Superman would remain comfortably, quietly, permanently quo.[20]

As such, Superman found itself increasingly in domestic situation-comedy scenarios which reflected the post-war status of American *masculinity*. While Superman comics covers depicted an actively martial Superman during the war years and slightly thereafter, postwar covers showed the opposite namely, Superman as a passive and awkward element in a domestic scene. This is exemplified by comparing the iconic cover of *Superman*, No. 233 (January, 1971), which symbolically depicts Superman as truly invincible, able to overcome all impediments including green kryptonite, the only controllable substance able to mortally wound it (albeit temporarily), with the cover of *Superman's Girl-Friend Lois Lane*, No. 112 appearing the same year, which shows Superman powerless to stop his bizarre arboreal transformation (see Figure 5 and Figure 6 below). This shift in characterisation mirrored the troubled attempts of war veterans to reintegrate into peace-time society and readjust to the duties involved in maintaining a household and a family.

This sense of being out of touch lead directly to widespread parody. Underground comics starring Gilbert Shelton's pornographic, super-powered Wonder Wart Hog, the World's Awfullest-Smelling Super-Hero, appeared in numerous humour magazines beginning in 1962. Similarly, NBC began airing an influential cartoon parody of Superman called *Underdog* on October 3, 1964. In March 1965, American Comics Group's Herbie morphed into the flying superhero the *Fat Fury*. The following month also saw Disney's Goofy became *Super Goof*. In October 1965, NBC aired the premiere episode of *Atom Ant*. Atom Ant's catchphrase was "Up and at 'em, Atom Aaaaaant!", parodying Superman's which was "Up, up, and Away!". Even Archie Andrews of Archie comics fame participated in Superman parodies by gaining superpowers and a form-fitting costume to fight crime on the placid streets of Riverdale. As a superhero, Archie operated under the moniker Pureheart the Powerful. Archie's supporting cast, Reggie, Betty, and Jughead, all adopted their own superheroic identities and soon afterwards were also indoctrinated into crime-fighting, parodying the now extensive Superman Family.

[20] G. Weldon, op. cit., p. 127.

Figure 5. Taken from *Superman*, Vol. 1, No. 233 (January, 1971). Written by Dennis O'Neil, illustrated by Curt Swan

Figure 6. Taken from *Superman's GirlFriend Lois Lane*, Vol. 1, No. 112 (August, 1971). Written by Carey Bates, illustrated by Werner Rot

Figure 7. Taken from *Superman's Girl-Friend Lois Lane*, Vol. 1, No. 19 (August, 1960). Written by Robert Bernstein, illustrated by Kurt Schaffenberger

Figure 8. Taken from Superman, Vol. 1, No. 166 (January, 1964). Written by Edmond Hamilton, illustrated by Curt Swan

There were animated Superman parodies as well: from *Super Chicken*, *The Mighty Heroes*, *Mighty Mouse*, to *Super President*. Included among these were also sitcom characters such as *Captain Nice* and *Mister Terrific*. Monty Python even parodied the super saturation of the Silver Age with their sketch titled "Bicycle Repairman," featuring a modest bicycle mechanic trying to make a living in a world inundated with superheroes. However, it was ABC's January 1966 *Batman* debut starring Adam West and Burt Ward as Batman and Robin respectively that made parody have a totally transformative effect on the concept of the comic book super-being in the eyes and imaginations of the public. In the wake of *Batman* (1966), the once dangerous and disruptive concept of the costumed hero was totally conflated with all things camp in a way that made the idea of a Superman or Batman equatable with farce and the abjectly absurd.[21] While Superman was still enjoying great success on radio, in comics, the character's fortunes had depreciated sharply. Sales of Superman comics were floundering in the face of Marvel comics' new-found dominance with psychologically complex and socially relevant characters like the neurotic Spider-Man, analogues for the socio-cultural problems of racial, ethnic, sexual, and religious discrimination in the X-Men, and the depiction of the tumultuous inter-relationships of a literally nuclear family in the Fantastic Four.

CONCLUSION

The end of the 1960s heralded the end of the what is conventionally known as The Silver Age of Comics for Superman. The time of rapid expansion of ideas, gimmicks, and new characters at the start of the decade had faded into mechanical repetition by its conclusion. While by the end of this period Superman was able to blow out distant stars with super-breath and withstand a thousand H-bombs without a scratch as depicted in *Adventure*, Vol. 1, No. 366 (March, 1968), the character's fantastical powers no longer matched the nation's darkening mood. As Knowles notes, "the social unrest of the Sixties terrified Middle America. As the civil rights movement went sour and industrial decay and urban blight created a new generation of increasingly vicious criminals, a new

---

[21]   Ibidem, pp. 135–139.

urban crime wave became" pre-eminent.[22] Superman's distant and lofty powers, which by this point were regarded largely as either tributary to the State or outrightly laughable, seemingly had no place or purpose in the prelude to the intense civil unrest witnessed in the drug related violence of the 1980s crack epidemic to come.

On the precipice of the sociopolitical, economic, cultural, and increasing ecological issues and debates that have become a seemingly intractable aspect of modern life, the figure of Superman can be described as confused, but also as impotent. The above analysis seemingly tracks a denouement in terms of the relationship between Otherness, power, and masculinity that can be thought of in two ways. On the one hand, the war-time truculence presented by the figure of Superman, as an emulative ideal, a herald and figurehead of jingoistic might and indomitability, could be described as limited to the remit of the war years. Moreover, the captivating expressions of this physical indomitability were more often than not also limited to the remit of the covers of *Superman* and *Action Comics* titles. As a result, one is lead to question whether the ending of the war necessarily diminished a space within which the excrescence of Superman's excessive power and Otherness could be both properly (that is, within and in support of the bounds of American standards of moral probity) and fully (that is, in open combat). If these expressions of war-winning power were limited to covers as they were, the latent superficiality of both display and the power it intimates suggests that both were, in some essential way, always-already performative.

On the other hand, I propose that a more severe denouement occurs in the progression of the figure of Superman during and after the war years. This decline or decay has less to do with the loss of masculine vitality, or the inability to discharge the character's male energy, whose fundamental alien Otherness precipitates levels of physical power that are, even in the midst of open modern warfare, extreme. Instead, the institutionalization of the character as an operation of the jingoistic ideology of the war, and the subsequent domestication of the character as a result of the conformist conservative ideology beginning in the 1950s – marked by anti-communist sentiments, the centrality of religious (specifically Judeo-Christian) faith, and unassailable patriotism – represents an essential loss of *potential* inherent to the character. In this milieu, the radical philosophical possibilities of a being as strong and

[22]   C. Knowles, op. cit., p. 154.

uncannily Other as Superman on Earth, as a figure of radical sociopolitical, economic, and cultural potential and change, are sublimated in favor of a conformist, and specifically American, identity. This identity is more man than alien, more American than Kryptonian, more terrestrial than intergalactic. In this way, the character's submits himself, his power, his Otherness and all the radical possibilities thereof, to the suburban ideal of Cold War Americana. On the cusp of the 90s, cold, too, is the question "well, whatever happened to the Man of Tomorrow?" Colder still is any exigency to provide an answer, nor belief in any answer provided.

BIBLIOGRAPHY

Bates C., Roth W., *Superman's Girl-Friend Lois Lane*, Vol. 1, No. 112, DC Comics, New York 1971.
Bernstein R., Schaffenberger K., *Superman's Girl-Friend Lois Lane*, Vol. 1, No. 19, DC Comics, New York 1960.
Cameron D., Citron S., *Superman*, Vol. 1, No. 34, DC Comics, New York 1945.
Cameron D., Dobrotka E., *Action Comics*, Vol. 1, No. 62, DC Comics, New York 1943.
Conroy M., *War Comics: A Graphic History*. Lewes: Ilex, 2009.
Darius J., *How Superman Would Win the War*, "Sequart" [www 01], http://sequart.org/magazine/23691/on-how-superman-would-win-the-war/ (accessed:13.06.2018).
Darowski J. J. T., *The Ages of Superman: Essays on the Man of Steel in Changing Times*, McFarland, Jefferson 2012.
Di Paolo M., *War, Politics and Superheroes: Ethics and Propaganda in Comics and Film* McFarland, Jefferson 2011.
Dobrotka E., *Action Comics*, Vol. 1, No. 76, DC Comics, New York 1944.
Finger B., Yarbrough I., *Superman*, Vol. 1, No. 26, DC Comics, New York 1944.
Hamilton E., Swan C., *Superman*, Vol. 1, No. 166, DC Comics, New York 1964.
Harrington W., *Superman and the War Years: The Battle of Europe Within the Pages of Superman Comics*. "The Superman Homepage", n.d. [www02], https://www.superman-homepage.com/comics/articles/supes-war.php.
Knowles C., *Our Gods Wear Spandex: The Secret History of Comic Book Heroes*, Weiser Books, San Francisco 2007.
Mangan J. A., *Shaping the Superman: Fascist Body as Political Icon – Aryan Fascism*, Routledge, London1999.
Mangan J. A., *Superman Supreme: Fascist Body as Political Icon – Global Fascism*, Routledge, London 1999.
O'Neil D., Swan C., *Superman*, Vol. 1, No. 233, DC Comics, New York 1971.
Plastino A., Bernstein R., *Adventure*, Vol. 1, No. 252, DC Comics, New York 1958.
Plastino A., Moore E., *Action Comics*, Vol. 1, No. 124, DC Comics, New York 1948.
Scott C., *Written in Red, White, and Blue: A Comparison of Comic Book Propaganda from World War II and September 11*, "The Journal of Popular Culture", Vol. 40, No. 2, 2007, pp. 325-343.

Seagle S. T., Kristiansen T. H., *It's A Bird...*, DC Comics, New York 2004.

Siegel J., Shuster J., *How Superman Would End The War*, "Look", 27th February, 1940.

Siegel J., Shuster J., *Superman*, Vol. 1, No. 17, DC Comics, New York 1942.

Siegel J., Shuster J., *Superman*, Vol. 1, No. 24, DC Comics, New York 1943.

Siegel J., Sikela J., *Action Comics*, Vol. 1, No. 47, DC Comics, New York 1942.

Siegel J., Nowak L., *Superman* Vol. 1, No. 13, DC Comics, New York 1941.

Siegel J., Nowak L., *Superman*, Vol. 1, No. 14, DC Comics, New York 1942.

Siegel J., Nowak L., *Superman*, Vol. 1, No. 16, DC Comics, New York 1942.

Siegel J., Nowak L., *Superman*, Vol. 1, No. 18, DC Comics, New York 1942.

Siegel J., Mortimer W., *Action Comics*, Vol. 1, No. 101, DC Comics, New York 1946.

Swan C., Hamilton E., *Superman*, Vol. 1, No. 156, DC Comics, New York 1962.

Swan C., Hamilton E., *Superman* Vol. 1, No. 164, DC Comics, New York 1963.

Swan C., Siegel J., *Superman's Pal, Jimmy Olsen*, Vol. 1, No. 53, DC Comics, New York 1961.

Swan C., Hamilton E., *Superman's Pal, Jimmy Olsen*, Vol. 1, No. 113, DC Comics, New York 1968.

Swan C., Dorfman L., *Superman*, Vol. 1, No. 162, DC Comics, New York 1963.

Swan C., Binder O., *Superman's Pal, Jimmy Olsen*, Vol. 1, No. 20, DC Comics, New York 1957.

Swan C., Binder O., *Superman's Pal, Jimmy Olsen* Vol. 1, No. 40, DC Comics, New York 1959.

Tye L., *Superman: A High-Flying History of America's Most Enduring Hero*, Random House, New York 2012.

The Press: Superman's Dilemma, "Time", 13th April, 1942.

Vaz M. C. *Tales of the Dark Knight*, Ballantine Books, New York 1989.

Weldon G., *Superman: The Unauthorized Biography*, Wiley, Hoboken, N.J. 2013.

Wright B. W., *Comic Book Nation. The Transformation of Youth Culture in America*, The Johns Hopkins University Press, Baltimore–London 2003.

RENATA IWICKA
http://orcid.org/0000-0001-6554-8841

REDEFINING NEW MASCULINITY IN KOREAN TELEVISION DRAMA SERIES

Abstract: This article mainly deals with the fictional male characters presented in Korean TV series aired in prime time (between 9:00PM and 12PM) and their gradual change. Author presents types of masculinity that permeates Korean society which presence is still felt in life (meninism movement) and compares them with new models of masculinity presented in recent years by writers for popular Kdramas. The shift is visible – the male hero changes from being a cold-hearted person healed by a female character, to a warm and supportive, asking for consent new model for sensitive masculinity. Television has the power to influence the viewers, the question remains – whether those who need the change the most watch those productions. However, after a barrage of Cold Prince copies, the change into a more multilayered, sensitive male character is visible.

Keywords: masculinity, South Korea, television series, fiction, Kdrama, sensitivity

In recent years, television products have become a powerful medium criticizing and analyzing the societal problems or various political issues even more boldly as in previous decades. Only the social media sites can rival, or even sometimes outdo, its power to influence the viewers. New modes of behavior and life models are shown through scripted characters to familiarize the audience with ideas previously either foreign or modified from the past ones. The societal changes researched here are only limited to the model of masculinity shown within the limits of the scripted television series, and the question whether it can or cannot affect the real-life behavior is tempting to answer. The main aim of this article is to show the connection between the changes in South Korea,[1] however slow they might seem to be, with the changes propagated, or proposed by TV series. A narrative analysis was conducted on chosen popular series and the results show the shift in the proposed models of masculinity, creating new, soft masculinity models.

1. METHODOLOGICAL SCOPE

As many voices called the current era a "Golden Age of Television", with this statement also comes a plethora of problems, mostly resulting from oversaturation of the market. In July of 2015, John Landgraf, Chairman of FX Network and FX Productions, coined the term 'peak TV' which has been used in countless news articles describing the state of 21st century television. He added that "[counting] TV shows is like counting lemmings. You can't even count the number of TV shows accurately. Hoping they won't run off a cliff and into an ocean."[2] And with more and more streaming platforms entering the market (like Disney+), the number of produced shows will be only rising – precisely to the peak after which the number will start to decline. This is still to be seen, however the voices that the "Golden Age of Television" is waning are starting to appear, taking under the consideration the growing popularity of the streaming services.[3] With this comes other issue that is often considered to be another factor (except for the sheer amount of shows that no one has enough time to watch) – namely the quality of the shows which will be declining with rising quantity. Some authors propose somewhat more optimistic outlook – for them with the diversification of platforms and with theme fragmentation also comes the quality of productions. In their "The New Yorker" article, Joshua Rothman and Erin Overbey sketch the

---

[1] Also referred simply as Korea within this text. For the transcript of Korean words there will be used the Revised Romanization (unless in quotations) and Korean names will follow the original pattern: family name first, given name second.

[2] N. Andreeva, *FX's John Landgraf Gives "Too Much TV" Update, Talks VOD Companies' Profitability, "Ridiculous" Lack Of Ratings Data – TCA*, https://deadline.com/2016/01/john-landgraf-too-much-tv-lemmings-streaming-viewership-data-1201684490/

[3] C. Ming, *The End of The Golden Age of Television and Why Content Is No Longer King*, https://christopherming.com/2018/04/end_of_golden_age_of_television_and_why_content_is_no_longer_king/.

history of "How TV Became Art," closing the article with the statement that reiterates this article's assumption that "[television] is still evolving, becoming more pervasive and personal. It will continue to change us in ways we can't foresee."[4]

1.1. SOUTH KOREAN TELEVISION

The South Korean television scene can be divided into two main categories – public broadcast companies (three largest being KBS, MBC, SBS) and cable television (like tvN, JTBC, OCN, Tv Chosun, MBN), not to mention various streaming platforms, and not counting Netflix, that produces and streams Korean content as well. Public broadcast companies are also bound by Broadcasting Act, which states in Article 5 (Public Responsibility of Broadcasting):

(1) A broadcast shall respect the dignity and value of human beings as well as the fundamental democratic order.

(2) A broadcast shall contribute to unifying the people, harmoniously developing the State, and forming the public opinion democratically, and shall not promote any discords among regions, generations, classes, and sexes.

(3) A broadcast shall not defame any third party's reputation or infringe on his or her rights.

(4) A broadcast shall not promote crimes, immoral conducts or a speculative spirit.

(5) A broadcast shall not promote lewdness, decadence or violence which has a negative influence on a sound family life and on a guidance of children and juveniles.[5]

The mission statement of all the public broadcasting companies emerges clear especially from the parts 4 and 5 – which also mean that behaviors or tropes presenting aforementioned issues cannot be shown as positive. This regulates, to a degree, the range of problems and issues

---

[4]   J. Rothman, E. Overbey, *How TV Became Art*, https://webcache.googleusercontent.com/search?q=cache:sytFtWud2eYJ:https://www.newyorker.com/culture/culture-desk/how-tv-became-art+&cd=14&hl=en&ct=clnk&gl=us.

[5]   *Broadcasting Act* [www01].

that can be touched upon during the drama. However, as with most guidelines, creative writing allows to circumvent or even eclipse these points. This is why Korean dramas from public broadcasters, no matter how bound by the Broadcasting Act, still can show certain issues without demonizing them or hiding them under the carpet. In recent years, the number of dramas that touch upon the issues of various kinds of inequality is rising. One of the most known examples of the clash between the attempt to include the topic of LGBT+ community was *Life Is Beautiful* drama (2010, SBS) which showed a gay couple without presenting both characters in any stereotypical way, but their relationship was somewhat "muted" and was not allowed the same level of intimacy that heterosexual couples enjoy. The drama was met with strong voices from the audience condemning showing such relationship, but the show did not yield to the negative comments too much, and did not erase the couple completely, even though the ending was, in a way, the outcome of the uproar.[6]

Cable broadcasting companies or streaming services produce dramas that place various issues regarding the society and also cultural norms if not at the center of the plot, then at least make them an important element in the plot overall. The issues that appear are various: majority of them deal with the corruption of various systems (political, judicial, or even critique of the media and even army), imbalance of power, the growing problems within the groups of adolescents (like prostitution, or crime), woman's place in the society, lately there has been a budding genre of BL (boys' love) webdramas, but they also present new types of characters in terms of both male and female leads. They are not as restrained as the public broadcasters, however they have to abide by some rules as well.[7] This does not mean that cable dramas are the land of the most progressive and cultural-norms-shattering productions, but they are more bold in pointing out the elements that do not work in Korean society, or those that should be talked about more often. It was JTBC drama *Just between Lovers* (2017) that introduced a disabled second lead character who did not serve as a mere break from the storyline of the main leads, but her own story, character, and romantic relationship was fully developed. This inclusivity was to show that Korean society is

---

[6]   Ibidem.
[7]   One of the most ridiculed by the audience is the blurring of sharp blades used as a weapon and deep, fatal wounds.

made from the vast array of people who are all equally valid, not only non-disabled characters. It familiarized the audience with the diversity, which is not only commendable but also badly needed. This is why since few years there has been a shift in male lead characters – from the cold and emotionally stunted person, who warms up only thanks to his love interest, to characters who display sensitivity from the start, and upend rigid gender norms or stereotypes in small but important steps.

It is often an overused statement, regarding the gender equality in South Korea, that much of the current situation is still influenced by Neo-Confucianism. This statement is both reductive and clouding the complex landscape of various factors contributing to the issue of gender inequality in contemporary Korean society. As Kim Seung-kyung and John Finch state: "Contemporary Korean Confucianism persists in family rituals practiced by many Koreans, but even more importantly in values and ethics that emphasize social stability and hierarchy, and which continue to structure important aspects of gender relations, work and family life."[8] Which only means that many of the tenets of Confucianism became "traditional" and not associated with any particular thought or philosophy. Of course, there is no denying that parts of gender bias stem from the Confucian roots (like confining women to the inner sphere of the house and therefore associating all household chores with "woman's work"[9]) however much of the today's misogyny has also current economic factors as one of the forces behind it – growing number of women in the workforce (although a very low percentage on management positions, not to mention the biggest wage gap among OECD countries[10]) is met with voices about "stealing" the work that should belong to men.[11] This became the most visible during the IMF crisis that hit Korea in 1997, rendering many men unemployed and forcing women to find work to support the family.

Sometimes the verbal aggression becomes physical violence and results in crimes – which is often the recurring theme in many dramas,

---

8   S. Kim, J. Finch, *Confucian Patriarchy Reexamined: Korean Families and the IMF Economic Crisis*, p. 43.
9   S. Sung, *Women Reconciling Paid and Unpaid Work in a Confucian Welfare State: The Case of South Korea*, pp. 342-360.
10   All data can be obtained through OECD website [www 04].
11   Such voices are heard during any of "men's right groups" that appear, especially the ones that target feminist organizations and groups such as Megalia (as seen in the short documentary: *South Korea's Gender Wars: Trolls, Threats and Anger Online* [www.06].

where the majority of the victims are women.[12] It is expected that women will stop working after the marriage, so more and more women push back the decision to get married or forego the process entirely, and this coupled with the country's low birthrate and high cost of childcare will result in the population shrinkage. The situation cannot be helped even with the paid maternity leave and one-month paternity leave (which was met with a strong opposition from the Ministry), even though already in 2011 a small survey proved that "[many] Korean male college students would consider being a stay-at-home dad if only society didn't frown on the role so much."[13] In the survey from Ministry of Gender Equality and Family almost 42% of the 3500 respondents answered that it's perfectly fine to be a "stay-at-home dad."[14] However, as Katrin Park (a former U.N. staffer, currently based in Seoul) writes in her opinion column: "When a male friend of mine, who works in a French luxury goods company's branch in Seoul, requested paternity leave, which he was entitled to, his boss asked him if he was the one giving birth. The Korean government's effort to mandate one-month paternity leave met with a fierce resistance last year within its own ministries on financial grounds."[15] There is also another legal problem – "stay-at-home fathers" cannot apply for the insurance as the Korean law does not recognize the husband as the traditional homemaker, which of course leads to financial worries as he is considered "unemployed." According to the National Statistical Office (NSO) review, the number of men "working on childcare and household chores among the economically inactive population stood at 156,000 as of last year (2019), up 20 percent from 130,000 in 2014."[16]

---

[12]   This was explicitly stated in the this year drama from OCN, *Missing: The Other Side*, where two characters who can see the dead, whose remains are not found, observe the surroundings and one of them points out that the majority of people who "live" there are women and children.

[13]   I. Nam, *Korean Men Willing to Tend Home, Survey Finds*, https://www.wsj.com/articles/ BL-KRTB-1807.

[14]   M. Kim, *New Types of Masculinity Represented in TV and Its Limitations: Focusing on Weekend Variety Programs*, p. 89.

[15]   K. Park, *S. Korea Reflects Lag in Gender Equality: Column*, https://eu.usatoday.com/story/ opinion/2015/03/14/womens-inequality-south-korea-park/70165200/.

[16]   J. Go, *A Man as a Stay-at-home Dad? – Male Homemakers Seen as Unemployed* ("남자가 전업주부라고요?"... '무직' 취급받는 남성 주부들), http://snaptime.edaily.co.kr/2020/ 09/%EB%82%A8%EC%9E%90%EA%B0%80-%EC%A0%84%EC%97%85%EC%A3%BC %EB%B6%80%EB%9D%BC%EA%B3%A0%EC%9A%94-%EB%AC%B4%EC%A7%81- %EC%B7%A8%EA%B8%89%EB%B0%9B%EB%8A%94-%EB%82%A8/ (in Korean).

With this in mind, it is important to add that many dramas do promote the changes, even if in an indirect manner – there are single fathers taking care of their children, husbands requesting the paternity leave, husbands/boyfriends who actually perform the duties usually associated with wives (like cooking, cleaning, child rearing), as well as male characters expressing they would prefer their future child to be a girl (which is an opposite to traditional Confucian preference).

1.2. HEGEMONIC AND SOFT MASCULINITY

Ever since the IMF crisis in 1997 a growing number of research was conducted on the shift in the Korean masculinity models with some, like Shin Kwang-yeong admitting that "[the] economic crisis transformed gender relations by reinforcing and undermining the patriarchal system at the same time."[17] This is equally true when analyzing drama characters – usually they are male-centric even if the male character represents the new type of masculinity. Dramas centered around women as the focal characters that are given the depth and variety of emotional states are still in the minority, even though the trend becomes visible (like the tvN production from 2019 – *Search: WWW*, having 3 main female leads with male counterparts treated almost like an accessory).[18]

The discourse on hegemonic masculinity owes much to both Gramsci's concept linking the hegemony to dominance of patriarchy, and Connell's research among Australian high school students. The later critique and further studies regarding the hegemonic masculinity, were still centered mostly around white, heterosexual, and Western males, but started to take other aspects under the consideration to propose a definition that could encompass as many factors important to the phenomenon as possible. As Terry A. Kupers writes:

In contemporary American and European culture, [hegemonic masculinity] serves as the standard upon which the "real man" is defined. According to [R. W.] Connell, contemporary hegemonic masculinity is built on

---

[17] K. Shin, *Asian Economic Crisis, Class and Patriarchy in Korean Society*, p. 1.
[18] This drama is also noteworthy for its portrayal of women having careers in highly competitive business – online news portals. Male characters here were not the agents propelling any significant changes in women's lives.

two legs, domination of women and a hierarchy of intermale dominance. It is also shaped to a significant extent by the stigmatization of homosexuality. Hegemonic masculinity is the stereotypic notion of masculinity that shapes the socialization and aspirations of young males. Today's hegemonic masculinity in the United States of America and Europe includes a high degree of ruthless competition, an inability to express emotions other than anger, an unwillingness to admit weakness or dependency, devaluation of women and all feminine attributes in men, homophobia, and so forth.[19]

The last statement is also true, to the degree, regarding the traditional male characters in Korean dramas as well – mostly the inability to express emotions or weakness, bouts of anger and other difficult emotions (like jealousy), displaying toughness, physical strength, possessiveness, often manifesting in a violent physical contact (like wrist-grabbing), but also such characteristics as: courage (the male hero will rescue the female lead) often bordering on bravado, athleticism (which is often shown through sequences of him doing sport or, indirectly, through shirtless scenes exposing his toned body), competitiveness (especially when the second male lead is involved), and achievement and success (the character is often a rich heir to some chaebol family). As the hegemonic masculinity exists only through relation – a subordinate form of masculinity is observed through the second lead, who can display similar traits but always to the lesser degree and with one crucial difference – the second lead is the emotional counterpart. And while M. Messner (and others, like A. Demetriou) analyses the "hybrid" or "soft" masculinities, he states that "[although] »softer« and more »sensitive« styles of masculinity are developing among some privileged groups of men, this does not necessarily contribute to the emancipation of women; in fact, quite the contrary may be true"[20] – but it is important to add that most of the research is about the white, heterosexual men, and therefore some findings or statements simply cannot be ascribed to Korean society and behavioral patterns. And while the majority of male characters in dramas (and even more in movies) can display macho traits as described above, according to Hofstede Index, Korea is considered to be a feminine society (39 points on the masculinity scale, to compare – Japan scores 95 on the same scale), which is further explained as:

---

[19]   T. A. Kupers, *Toxic Masculinity as a Barrier to Mental Health Treatment in Prison*, p. 716.
[20]   M. Messner, *'Changing Men' and Feminist Politics in the United States*, p. 725.

A low score (Feminine) on the dimension means that the dominant values in society are caring for others and quality of life. A Feminine society is one where quality of life is the sign of success and standing out from the crowd is not admirable.[21]

The fundamental issue here is what motivates people, wanting to be the best (Masculine) or liking what you do (Feminine).

South Korea scores 39 on this dimension and is thus considered a Feminine society. In Feminine countries the focus is on "working in order to live," managers strive for consensus, people value equality, solidarity and quality in their working lives. Conflicts are resolved by compromise and negotiation. Incentives such as free time and flexibility are favoured. Focus is on well-being, status is not shown. An effective manager is a supportive one, and decision making is achieved through involvement.[22]

In this aspect "soft" masculinity used in this text does not conform to the proposed definitions above. It is only used as an adjective contrary to "hard" or "dominant" masculinity displayed by many male characters purely because of the lack of a better term. "Dominant masculinity" or "assertive masculinity" might be the terms that describes the behavior of the male leads more accurately as it often happens that such a lead chooses clothes for the female lead, decides on some changes in her life – not to the toxic level displayed by Christian Grey, but the assertion of power is still visible – especially serving as the warning sign to the second lead, claiming the ownership over the female lead.

The analysis of masculinity concept proposed by Baek Seongi and Kim Nam-il points to the shift in the concept – in the second half of the 90's, which coincides with the financial crisis, to a "permissive masculinity" (허여적 남성성), that incorporates traditionally feminine attributes.[23] It is worthy to add that the second half of the same decade is also the beginning of change in the Korean music scene (Seo Taiji And The Boys, as well as H.O.T.) which also started to influence the change in the dominant cultural norms. As early as in 2005, SBS aired a series called *Bad*

---

[21]   *Hofstede Insights* [www03].
[22]   Ibidem.
[23]   After: M. Kim, op. cit., p. 91.

Housewife, that reversed the traditionally allotted gender roles – in here it is the male character who retires and stays home, and his wife becomes the breadwinner for the family. Such settings is in fact, nothing extraordinary to Kdrama array of plotlines.

The analysis will be based on television series chosen for representing the shift in the new model in the most explicit way perceivable. It is sufficient to add that there are other series, omitted from this study, in which this new model of masculinity may be also visible. This study will focus only on television drama productions, therefore the movies will not be included, as well as any variety shows.[24] The dramas showing such characters were chosen from the 2017 to 2020 as the change was the most visibly in the productions from this time bracket. Majority of the shows belong to the "romantic comedy" category, however in Korean case, this genre incorporates also other characteristics from different groups. Romantic comedy is also one of the genres that is almost equal in the gender representation (having a male and a female leads, their circles of friends and families, complementary second leads, etc.). It is also the genre that is most accused of stereotyping and enforcing the stereotypes, this is why it would be beneficial to present it as the vehicle of change in perceived stereotypes and proposing new models of behavior. It is important to add that this research into the characters proposed by the tv series might be about the transient model, because next seasons could propose something else entirely.

2. FROM ARROGANCE TO SENSITIVITY

2.1. "THE RICH JERK"

For a significant portion of the past decade, Korean dramas were populated with male leads who, at the beginning of the plot, were cold, often cruel in a haughty way, and often obnoxious. With time, after meeting the female lead, they started to shed this image to fully become, if not

---

[24] There is a significant research into the masculinity models in movies and also in variety shows, much less is available on the drama representation of it. As examples out of the wide research may serve: A. Lee, *Traumatized Masculinity in Jung Jiwoo's Happy End*, pp. 169-194; M. Kim, op. cit., p. 88-96.

a good guy, then at least not as terrible. The standard dramas of this kind are *Full House* (2004, KBS2) and ever more *Boys Over Flowers* (2008)[25] where the main male character was an obnoxious, pampered, and spoiled son of a prestigious family, who bullied and belittled others. However, as the plot progressed, he learned the values of care and love. The softness and caring about other people's needs were the characteristics of the second male lead, who often understood the female lead's predicaments, troubles, and served as the proverbial "shoulder to cry on." This situation is not, of course, unique to Korean drama only – it appears within the genres of various cultural products, from books, comics to movies, also from other countries. Additionally – not every male lead fell into this category – there still were dramas with sensitive and nice male characters, just as now there are also still "rich jerks" as the main leads.

This model of dominant masculinity coincided with the rapid proliferation of Korean cultural products after the success of *Boys Over Flowers*. It is important to note that in the pre-*BOF* era, a male lead who expressed his sensitivity was also featured in the dramas.[26] It is only later that the sentimental leading man was replaced by "a cold jerk" as the main character trope. The aggressive promotion of Hallyu (that is Korean Wave) found its embodiment in the male lead. The male leads in such titles as: *You're Beautiful* (2009, SBS), *Secret Garden* (2010, SBS), *Playful Kiss* (2010, MBC), *Heartstrings* (2011, MBC), *The Master's Sun* (2013, SBS), *My Love From the Star* (2013-2014, SBS),[27] *Fated to Love You* (2014, MBC), *Cinderella and the Four Knights* (2016, tvN), *Madame Antoine* (2016, JTBC) *I'm Not a Robot* (2017-2018, MBC), *What's Wrong with Secretary Kim* (2018, tvN), may be considered as cold or even antisocial. They often hold a well-respected job or they are the chaebol heirs, and this aspect is often a critique of real life chaebol sons and daughters, who are far removed from the realities of ordinary people, and their privileged

[25] Aired on KBS, directed by Jeon Kisang. It is yet another version of the Japanese manga of the same title. Before the Korean version, Taiwanese and Japanese live series were also produced.

[26] The most famous example is of course drama *Winter Sonata* (2002, KBS2) and the character played by Bae Yongjun, whose popularity skyrocketed in Japan, nearly singlehandedly starting the local Hallyu. This drama is given as the starting point of the first wave of K-drama popularity outside of Korea. It is also featured almost in every research regarding Hallyu phenomenon.

[27] In here the male lead is an alien, so that might be an excuse for his cold demeanor.

and arrogant behavior makes for scandals erupting from time to time.[28] The bad behavior of Kdrama chaebols is usually redeemed with their latest development and character growth. This may call into question the motivation of such change – usually it happens because the rude man encounters a warm, even if a bit naïve, or adorably clumsy woman, who often does not belong to the same social strata. I would disagree, however, about comparing such stories to Cinderella, as it is often done both by misinformed researchers and even the audience. First and the biggest difference is that Cinderella is not entirely the agent of her own story – anything of importance, that happens in her life, is the result of other people's intervention and she becomes the collateral, while the Kdrama female lead is often portrayed as a self-reliant, stubborn person who perseveres through troubled times (which may be seen as the passive trait sometimes), but also initiates the action that can change her life. The best example of such character is the heroine of this year's (2020) KBS2 drama *Into the Ring* – exasperated with being treated like a pest, Gu Sera decides to go into the local politics to bring change for the community.[29]

Male leads who undergo the change from the cold-hearted jerk to the doting boyfriend serve not only as one part of show's dynamic. They also illustrate two important factors. First – it shows that nothing is impossible, as long as a person is willing to change. The problematic aspect is in the vehicle of such change – if a male lead changes only because of the woman he meets, how deep the change really is? This immediately leads to another question – would he remain an arrogant brat had he not met the warm and caring female lead? The problem arises when the answer is positive. This may mean that even if the lead changes and

---

[28] This is also true regarding every privileged person towards their subordinates, such entitled behavior may lead to *gapjil* – a neologism describing an abuse of one's power especially by those who are of position of power over the subordinates. Such behavior is criticized and looked down on, as the recent incidents prove (now (in)famous "nut rage" of the Korean Air vice president Cho Hyeon-ah, or the "authoritarian no-look pass" of the politician Kim Museong, and even the latest scandal involving Red Velvet's member Irene).

[29] It would be tempting to conduct the study on female representation in Korean series along the levels of gender stereotyping like *recognition* and *respect*. After: S. Daalmans, M. Kleemans, A. Sadza, *Gender Representation on Gender-Targeted Television Channels: A Comparison of Female- and Male-Targeted TV Channels in the Netherlands*, pp. 366–378, https://doi.org/10.1007/s11199-016-0727-6.

starts to see people around him as the actual people and not servants, the work on his own character cannot stop here because it does not penetrate his personal world view or family upbringing and values. Second factor goes beyond the screen – it may give the viewers the hope that a) finding such partner is possible, or b) the change in the characters of their current partners is possible, especially when the relationship is far from the perfect. The implications of such view, however, are not in the scope of this article.

2.2. COLD OUTSIDE FLUFF INSIDE

The hybrid character of another type of a male lead is the transition that helped to facilitate the appearance of the sensitive male leads. This hybrid character means that the lead behaves in a distant or stoical way, but in fact under the frozen surface there is an ocean of sensitivity. Such characters cannot be treated as openly rude and actively engaging in abusive behavior (verbally or physically), but they are not openly warm either, at least not until a certain point in their lives. With such characters the writers can present a variety of social and cultural issues, as well as taboos. This may be visible in the male leads from such dramas like: *It's Okay, That's Love* (2014, SBS), *Just Between Lovers* (2017, JTBC), *A Poem a Day* (2018, tvN), *Her Private Life* (2019, tvN), *Into the Ring* (2020, KBS2), *It's Okay to Not Be Okay* (2020, tvN), and more. In this case, changing of the character also comes from the relationship, however the emotional landscape of the male leads is shaped not by their elevated economical background, but an event that led them to the temporal inability to express feelings directly. This event might range from the love affair gone awry or a personal trauma[30] – with resolving this issue and working on the psychological issues, the male lead can revert back to his previous, emotional nature. This model differs from the previous, because the "rich jerk" does not have the base to which he can go back to, except for the childhood, misconstrued through

[30] In the sense proposed by *Substance Abuse and Mental Health Services Administration as:* "Individual trauma results from an event, series of events, or set of circumstances that is experienced by an individual as physically or emotionally harmful or threatening and that has lasting adverse effects on the individual's functioning and physical, social, emotional, or spiritual well-being." See [www 07].

memories and often spent in an emotionally cold environment. Only after opening up and warming up thanks to the female lead, he starts to build his own "emotional bank."

The move from the emotionally blocked to sensitive is less dramatic within such character, even if the reason of the block was a certain trauma. The healing provided through the course of the episodes, started by the fateful meeting with another person, draws on the lead's own ability to process complicated feelings and overcome the traumatic memories.

2.3. SENSITIVE LEADS

The most interesting characters, displaying new models of the masculinity can be found in such series as: *Temperature of Love* (2017, SBS), *My Mister* (2018, tvN), *Catch the Ghost* (2019, tvN), *One Spring Night* (2019, MBC), *Extraordinary You* (2019, MBC), *Tale of Nokdu* (2019, KBS2/Wavve), *When the Weather Is Fine* (2020, JTBC), *365: Repeat the Year* (MBC, 2020). Positive characters are usually viewed as bland and uninteresting, and it is easy to infer that viewers prefer complicated characters – which are usually reserved for scheming adversaries of the heroes. It is much harder to create an interesting and engaging character who could be considered "a good guy." Of the examples of the proposed new sensitive masculinity is the male lead of *Temperature of Love*, Oh Jeong-seon, who aspires to become a Chef one day. He expresses his feelings without much reservation and yet is always aware of the space that should be allowed to another person. The difference between his behavior and that of the earlier discussed models shows in two, very important scenes. In first, when leaning to kiss, he asks for permission. He informs about his intentions and gives the female lead time to either refuse or accept. This asking for a consent, especially early in the relationship is still a rare sight in dramas (and not only Korean ones). The other moment showing his attitude to emotionality is his statement in one episode that anyone can cry if they're sad, regardless of gender. This may not be anything groundbreaking within the Kdrama framework where male leads are often seen crying, however this statement goes beyond the female lead with whom he was talking at that time. This echoes the term mentioned earlier – the "permissive masculinity," incorporating the traditionally ascribed female behavior like crying[31] and normalizing it as the human response, and not gendered one. As Mothro et al., states:

> While adult crying occurs across both sexes (…) we argue that crying is much more fitting for individuals who are perceived to possess communal (e.g., gentle, vulnerable) rather than agentic (e.g., powerful, dominant) characteristics. As a man is supposed to be powerful and dominant, the act of crying (which connotes helplessness, vulnerability, and weakness) violates our perceptions of his typical societal role. Research provides support for our arguments and the notion that a crying man is seen as atypical. Popular sayings like "boys don't cry" and "crying is for girls" (…) reinforce the presence of societal norms regarding gender and crying behavior.[32]

This is why it is important to not only see the male characters crying, which after some time may seem like a staple, but also hear male characters asserting that it is OK to cry because this is just a normal human reaction.

Yet another example of a slightly different sensitivity is the male lead in *One Spring Night* – Yu Jiho who is a single father relying also on his parents' help in raising his son. With time the viewers learn that the mother of the child has left right after the boy was born and never returned or even enquired after him. Therefore, when the contact is made, Jiho falls apart at the thought that she will come and take the child from him. In this drama, that deals with many seemingly trivial issues, the biological mother is almost completely absent, and yet not even Jiho condemns her. He excuses her behavior, explaining that they were young then and accidental pregnancy felt like a life sentence to her. Which is also one of the moments that general public should hear more often – that sometimes women are not ready to be mothers and that they should not be blamed for refusing the motherhood. Single parenting made Jiho into a social outcast – he himself is sure that no woman will ever want to start a relationship with him because he is a single father. This made him both shutting from the eventual meetings and yet from this voluntary solitude grew his deep need to

---

[31] D. Motro, A. P. J. Ellis, *Boys, Don't Cry: Gender and Reactions to Negative Performance Feedback*, pp. 227–235, https://doi.org/10.1037/apl0000175.
[32] Ibidem, p. 225.

feel love again. This is why when he meets a woman who is apparently undeterred by the fact he is a single father, he jumps into the relationship with everything that he is, except he is not willing to sacrifice his son's dignity. The drama finds the balance between the eager start of a new relationship (Jiho is also reluctant as he does not want a nanny for his child, as he explains, but also a partner for himself) and respect for a child.

Two dramas from the list do not have the love relationship in the traditional sense (*My Mister* and *365: Repeat the Year*), but display two distinct models of masculinity – one is mature and supportive, the other shows the male lead whose character traits are usually ascribed to female leads – he is bright, optimistic, unabashed in showing fanboy[33] attitude, and believes in other people, despite being a detective. Park Donghun from *My Mister* represents the silent portion of his middle-aged generation – with every expectation that was placed upon them, with disappointments (coming from both work and private life). He may not have any money related problems (contrary to the female lead) but still his life feels like a life wasted and only through the non-romantic relationship with Yi Jian that they both start to see the life ahead and around them differently. They both can be seen as "losers," unable to stand up to people who abuse them physically or psychologically, and yet they still fight to remain humas. Park Donghun remains kind, empathetic and supportive not only to his own family but to strangers as well. And this quiet kindness and reaching out to help other people is precisely the kinds of traits that are needed.

The three dramas mentioned here, that is *Catch the Ghost, Extraordinary You* and *When the Weather is Fine,* share one common characteristic displayed by the male leads. All of them are of course kind and helpful, sometimes at their own expense, but they are also on the patient side of the relationship. This is especially seen within Im Eunseob from *When the Weather Is Fine.* His life is just a passive existence stuck between insomnia, blog writing and book club meetings organized in his bookstore. He is a person that everyone in the tiny town depends on – be it helping with various menial tasks, rescuing people lost in the mountainous forest or organizing the book club evenings that provide a repose from the everyday worries. When one winter Mok Hyewon

---

[33]   The word is used in a positive and not derogatory sense to mean an enthusiast.

comes to her hometown, Eunseob remains collected, not giving himself any hope that this winter would be any different. Mok Hyewon treats the town as the repose whenever life in Seoul feels too much of a burden for her, plagued with an emotional freeze after an incident in high school that left her vulnerabilities exposed and bullied. Her presence forces Eunseob to confront his feelings for her he kept hidden since the high school, but at the same time his quiet and warm personality starts to thaw her icy and indifferent behavior. Eunseob is highly intuitive and does not act on impulses, with few exceptions. Everything he does for others he does without expecting any gratitude, not expecting he is worthy of people's affection. His personality allows him to wait for Hyewon and her decision, and what more – he respects her need to be alone, to have her own space (physical and mental). His character is as far from the cold jerks as it can be.

In *Extraordinary You* the whole plot was the parody of typical comic book stories marketed to female readers. Which allowed to create a male lead out of the role of the statist – who in comic books are drawn without any features, lines or even names, but they serve just as the background for main characters. This in turn allowed to fill his traits with characteristics usually associated with the second lead. As they were characters in the comic book themselves, this trick also proved useful in creating his counterpart – a typical rich jerk. Haru displayed all of the modes possessed by the second leads: he was empathetic, caring, honorable. But more than that – he listened to the female lead and did not pressure or threaten her. He embodied what is felt today to be lacking from the female environment – a safety.

Similar safety and empathy was displayed by Go Jiseok, a male lead from *Catch the Ghost*. This drama, in the deceptively light format presented many societal issues that needs to be addressed. Just at the very beginning the plot was filled with the crime regarding *molka* – that is a hidden camera installed in secret to spy on unsuspecting women, often during sexual encounters.[34] Without any break yet another issue was presented – a disguised version of the scandal that erupted in 2018 and is known today as the "Burning Sun scandal" – that exposed the sexual violence, misogyny and abuse of power, involving many celebrities and

---

[34] K. Neetha, *South Korea 'Molka' Sex Scandal: As More Horrors are Revealed the Country's Sex Crime Problem is Laid Bare*, https://meaww.com/molka-scandal-telegram-nth-room-south-korea-needs-to-do-more-combat-sex-crimes-against-women-girls.

police officers.[35] Allusions to both *molka* and Burning Sun appeared in various dramas, also followed by characters who expressed their abhorrence for sexual violence (like Oh Yangchon from the drama *Live*, about the police, 2018, tvN). *Catch the Ghost* offered even more issues that sometimes are too uncomfortable for the mainstream dramas: like taking care of people with mental disabilities and the psychological effects it can have on their guardians, as well the problem of elderly people who suffer from various ailments associated with the old age – in this case it was dementia. Jiseok's patience and empathy stemmed from the fact he had to take care of his mother who suffered from the dementia, mentally stuck in her early twenties. He understood how tiresome such care can be. He was able to extend his empathy to other people, himself not demanding anything from others.

One of the motifs that allows for blurring the boundaries and exploring the inner workings of the "opposite sex" is *gender bender* plot solution which is used from time to time in dramas for various purposes. It is done by mostly girls pretending to be boys for various reasons such as: getting or keeping a job (*Coffee Prince* 2007, MBC; *You're Beautiful* 2009 SBS), getting into the Confucian university (*Seongkyunggwan Scandal* 2010, KBS2), school (*To the Beautiful You* 2012, SBS), or providing for the family (*Scholar Who Walks the Night* 2015, MBC or *Moonlight Drawn by Clouds* 2016, KBS2). And usually it leaves no trace of any influence on the person undergoing the whole process. The character can move back from the assumed male identity to woman's without any problem or lingering effects that would display in behavior. With this aspect in mind, the drama *The Tale of Nokdu* (2019, KBS2/Wavve) is quite different. In here it is the male lead who pretends to be a woman.[36] He not only behaves like a woman when "in the role," he also displays traits usually associated with female gender both before and after his temporary gender switch (like empathy, care, compassion,

[35] K. Sonia, *K-Pop Crime Cartel Revealed as Korea's Burning Sun Scandal Expands*, https://variety.com/2019/music/asia/korea-burning-sun-scandal-reveals-a-k-pop-crime-cartel-1203174904/. The most comprehensive timeline of the complicated issue is presented on Wikipedia: [www 02].

[36] I do not count the motif of "body swap", therefore no *Secret Garden* on the list. Also excluding *Ma Boy* (2012, Tooniverse) as too short (3 episodes) even though it features rare *gender bender* motif of a boy pretending to be a girl.

sensitivity[37]). He admits he learned how hard is the women's life, how much prejudice they are met with, and how neglected and expendable their lives are. In here, the brief switch does not end with the first half of the drama – in the last episode there is a scene in which the titular Nokdu, the protagonist, dons the woman's *hanbok* once again to lure and punish those who commit crimes against women (he says in one episode, with utter disgust, that he hates men who harm women while beating up a perpetrator of such crime).

What is even more noteworthy – the action takes place in 1614, only mere years after the Japanese invasion (*Imjin waeran*) which left the country in ruins. And there is another storm brewing on the horizon – the growing Qing forces that will destroy the Ming Dynasty and will wage attacks on Joseon as well. This timeframe allowed the screenwriter to explore societal problems that are also relevant in the 21st century, mostly the lives of women of different classes who had to overcome traumatic events in their lives. And this points to the stigma of rape which in many countries is still a pervasive problem.[38] The stigma related to rape leads to the crime being underreported.[39]

The male hero does not work as the sole savior of the women here, he transcends even further – he becomes one of them, which allows him to not only see but also experience a woman's life himself. Then he understands their everyday hardships and past traumas, which in turn allows him to never become patronizing. This also allows him to reach to his own sensitivity unabashed, without any reservations about

---

[37] More about the stereotypical gender traits in: *Encyclopedia of Women and Gender, Two-Volume Set: Sex Similarities and Differences and the Impact of Society on Gender.*

[38] This might or might not hint at sexual violence and crimes committed during any conflict in 21st century, but in the drama the survivors of sexual violence founded a secretive Women's Village, where no man could enter, serving as a sanctuary, providing the healing environment and self-sustaining in the terms of economy. It was later destroyed and almost all women killed, as if a grim reminder that no sphere cannot be excluded from the male dominance. In this subplot it is indirectly exploited the need of a more extensive help program to the victims of sexual violence – just as explicitly stated by members of the UN during the meeting in 2017. *Shame, Stigma Integral to Logic of Sexual Violence as War Tactic, Special Adviser Tells Security Council, as Speakers Demand Recognition for Survivors*, https://www.un.org/press/en/2017/sc12819.doc.htm.

[39] WHO states that "about 1 in 3 (35%) of women worldwide have experienced either physical and/or sexual intimate partner violence or non-partner sexual violence in their lifetime." Which also includes not reported cases, as the numbers indicated by reported cases show: *Rape Statistics by Country 2020* [www05].

his behavior and rules stating that men should not be affectionate or show emotions. Nokdu clearly shows that such statements are just artificial constructs, limiting and hurting the person who tries to adhere to the rigid societal and cultural norms. His unrestrained sensitivity is met with Dongju's restraint stemming from her own personal trauma and inability to show or even acknowledge affection. His character shows that there is no such thing as inherently feminine or masculine character traits and that could make the male audience express and show their feelings without feeling guilty of negatively perceived "effeminate" behavior. It shows that sensitivity is human trait, regardless of gender.[40] Jang Dongyun who portrayed Nokdu said during an interview:

> Through my role, I was able to experience what kind of social pressure those women had to go through. Yet I still feel there are remnants of injustice left in our current society, and there is a lot that needs to be changed. (…) I paid extra attention to not making my role seem humorous and tried to exaggerate my voice to make it sound like that of a woman. (…) Cross-gender acting has been off limits in Korean TV shows or movies for a long time, but people have just begun to open up discussions about it. People nowadays are open-minded about cross-gender roles without limiting their performances to the gender they were born with. In my case, by taking this role, it became a turning point for me to become an actor without being trapped in the gender frame.[41]

CONCLUSION

Drawing from many examples analyzed above, it becomes visible that the new models of masculinities proposed by drama series are, if not prevalent, then at least a growing, tendency to portray the male lead differently than in many previous, well known works. The traits that

---

[40] *Gender bender* is close but not identical to transgender identity. It is a temporary transgression, similar to the temporal transgender roles played by Korean shamans during rituals.

[41] H. Jung, *TV Shows, Stage Productions Embrace Diverse Roles for Men*, https://www.koreatimes.co.kr/www/art/2020/08/688_279702.html.

appear more often were usually associated with female characters: soft-ness, vulnerability, sensitivity, compassion, empathy. The dramas ana-lyzed were both from public and cable broadcast companies and even though the cable dramas delved deeper into various societal issues, both presented new models of masculinities. They rest primarily on the sen-sitivity that can be reached and thus creating – still fictional – model for real life behavior. Which is also helped by real life influential figures who are not afraid to speak about the sensitivity as one of the virtues in one's life. Kim Jonghyeon, asked what he would wish for if granted a wish replied: "I would wish for an emotional sensitivity that never runs dry."[42] And we can only hope that tv dramas, having the power to influence the audience, will try further to explore different modes of masculinity.

BIBLIOGRAPHY

Andreeva N., *FX's John Landgraf Gives "Too Much TV" Update, Talks VOD Companies' Profit-ability, "Ridiculous" Lack Of Ratings Data – TCA*, https://deadline.com/2016/01/john-land-graf-too-much-tv-lemmings-streaming-viewership-data-1201684490/ (accessed: 12.11.2020).

Daalmans S., Kleemans M., Sadza A., *Gender Representation on Gender-Targeted Televi-sion Channels: A Comparison of Female- and Male-Targeted TV Channels in the Nether-lands*. "Sex Roles", No. 77, 2017, pp. 366–378, https://doi.org/10.1007/s11199-016-0727-6 (accessed: 12.11.2020).

Encyclopedia of Women and Gender, Two-Volume Set: Sex Similarities and Differences and the Impact of Society on Gender, J. Worell (ed.), Academic Press, Cambridge 2001.

Go J., *A Man as a Stay-at-home Dad? – Male Homemakers Seen as Unemployed* ("남자가 전업주부라고요?"... '무직' 취급받는 남성 주부들), http://snaptime.edaily.co.kr/20-20/09/%EB%82%A8%EC%9E%90%EA%B0%80-%EC%A0%84%EC%97%85%EC%A3%B-C%EB%B6%80%EB%9D%BC%EA%B3%A0%EC%9A%94-%EB%AC%B4%EC%A7%81-%EC%B7%A8%EA%B8%89%EB%B0%9B%EB%8A%94-%EB%82%A8/ (in Korean) (ac-cessed: 12.11.2020).

Jung H., *TV Shows, Stage Productions Embrace Diverse Roles for Men*, https://www.korea-times.co.kr/www/art/2020/08/688_279702.html (accessed: 12.11.2020).

Kim M., *New Types of Masculinity Represented in TV and Its Limitations: Focusing on Weekend Variety Programs* ("TV매체에 재현된 새로운 남성성(masculinity)과 그 한계 -주말 예능프로그램을 중심으로-), "Journal of Korea Contents Association", Vol. 14, No. 1, 2014, pp. 88–96 (in Korean).

Kim S., Finch J., *Confucian Patriarchy Reexamined: Korean Families and the IMF Economic Crisis*, "The Good Society", Vol. 1, No. 3, 2002, pp. 43–49.

---

[42] From twitter user: Words by Jjong, @wordsbyjjong: https://twitter.com/wordsbyjjong/status/1326901397506428930.

Kupers T. A., *Toxic Masculinity as a Barrier to Mental Health Treatment in Prison*, "Journal of Clinical Psychology", Vol. 61, No. 6, 2005, pp. 713-724.

Lee A., *Traumatized Masculinity in Jung Jiwoo's Happy End*, "The Review of Korean Studies", Vol. 19, No.1, 2016, pp. 169-194.

Messner M., *'Changing Men' and Feminist Politics in the United States*, "Theory and Society", Vol. 22, No. 5, 1993, pp. 723-737.

Ming C., *The End of The Golden Age of Television and Why Content is No Longer King*, https://christopherming.com/2018/04/end_of_golden_age_of_television_and_why_content_is_no_longer_king/ (accessed: 12.11.2020).

Motro D., Ellis A. P. J., *Boys, Don't Cry: Gender and Reactions to Negative Performance Feedback*, "Journal of Applied Psychology", Vol. 102, No. 2, 2017, pp. 227–235. https://doi.org/10.1037/apl0000175 (accessed: 12.11.2020).

Neetha K., *South Korea 'Molka' Sex Scandal: As More Horrors are Revealed the Country's Sex Crime Problem is Laid Bare*, https://meaww.com/molka-scandal-telegram-nth-room-south-korea-needs-to-do-more-combat-sex-crimes-against-women-girls (accessed: 12.11.2020).

Nam I., *Korean Men Willing to Tend Home, Survey Finds*, https://www.wsj.com/articles/BL-KRTB-1807, 25th April, 2011 (accessed: 12.11.2020).

Nugroho S. A., *The Ending Scenes of Korean Gay-Themed Movies and TV Dramas: A Perpetual View of Korean Society Towards Homosexuality?*, https://www.academia.edu/2358676/The_Ending_Scenes_of_Korean_Gay_Themed_Movies_and_TV_Dramas_A_Perpetual_View_of_Korean_Society_Towards_Homosexuality (no information on publishing details) (accessed: 12.11.2020).

Park K., *S. Korea Reflects Lag in Gender Equality: Column*, https://eu.usatoday.com/story/opinion/2015/03/14/womens-inequality-south-korea-park/70165200/ (accessed: 12.11.2020).

Rothman J., Overbey E., *How TV Became Art*, https://webcache.googleusercontent.com/search?q=cache:sytFtWud2eYJ:https://www.newyorker.com/culture/culture-desk/how-tv-became-art+&cd=14&hl=en&ct=clnk&gl=us (accessed: 12.11.2020).

Shame, Stigma Integral to Logic of Sexual Violence as War Tactic, Special Adviser Tells Security Council, as Speakers Demand Recognition for Survivors, UN Security Council, 7938th Meeting (AM), 15th May 2017, https://www.un.org/press/en/2017/sc12819.doc.htm (accessed: 12.11.2020).

Shin K., *Asian Economic Crisis, Class and Patriarchy in Korean Society*, "The International Scope", Vol. 3, No. 5, 2001, pp. 1-17.

Sonia K., *K-Pop Crime Cartel Revealed as Korea's Burning Sun Scandal Expands*, https://variety.com/2019/music/asia/korea-burning-sun-scandal-reveals-a-k-pop-crime-cartel-1203174904/ (accessed: 12.11.2020).

Sung S., *Women Reconciling Paid and Unpaid Work in a Confucian Welfare State: The Case of South Korea*, "Social Policy & Administration", No. 37, 2003, pp. 342-360.

Words by Jjong: @wordsbyjjong: https://twitter.com/wordsbyjjong/status/1326901397506428930 (accessed: 12.11.2020).

Internet sources

Broadcasting Act [www 01], https://elaw.klri.re.kr/eng_service/lawView.do?hseq=38778&lang=ENG (accessed: 12.11.2020).

Burning Sun Scandal [www 02], https://en.wikipedia.org/wiki/Burning_Sun_scandal (accessed: 12.11.2020).

Hofstede Insights [www 03], https://www.hofstede-insights.com/country-comparison/south-korea/.

OECD website [www04], https://www.oecd-ilibrary.org/.

Rape Statistics by Country 2020 [www05], https://worldpopulationreview.com/country-rankings/rape-statistics-by-country.

South Korea's Gender Wars: Trolls, Threats and Anger Online [www 06], https://www.youtube.com/watch?v=gy4oFVuNPkg).

Substance Abuse and Mental Health Services Administration [www 07], https://web.archive.org/web/20140805161505/http://www.samhsa.gov/traumajustice/traumadefinition/definition.aspx.

KSENIA OLKUSZ

http://orcid.org/0000-0002-6620-4300

STRIPPING THE VAMPIRE. EROTIC IMAGINATIONS AND SEXUAL FANTASIES IN PARANORMAL ROMANCES (A STUDY OF SELECTED EXAMPLES)[1]

Abstract: In paranormal romances, one can witness a significant transformation of a vampire from a multifaceted monstrosity into the figure of an adorer who becomes an object of desire, fascination, and an object of erotic imagining. This very transition seems to have been triggered by a shift in the literary convention regarding vampires. So, it no longer contributes to a typical gothic narrative, but to a form of romance seasoned with a little fantasy, thereby depriving this archetypical blood-sucker of their nefarious image and qualifying them unequivocally as adorers. In that regard, any traditional means of defining vampirism become secondary to those less associated with gothic and more with romance narratives. Consequently, vampiric sexuality emerges as a substantial part of the plot, along with descriptions of physical intercourses that are even wont to verge on pornography.

Keywords: paranormal romance, vampires, sexuality, pornography, romance, gothic narratives

Paranormal romance is a variant of romantic narrative with elements of fantasy and as such has been popular since the beginning of the 21st century, but its sources date to the preceding one. Leigh M. McLennon writes:

---

[1]   Polish version of this paper was published in "Orbis Linguarum" (2015).

Although it emerged only in the 1990s, (…) and paranormal romance genre now exerts a powerful influence on representations of monsters and the supernatural in popular culture. Over the last 25 years or so, urban fantasy and paranormal romance (hereafter abbreviated as UF/PR) has developed into a new, easily recognisable genre formula: sympathetic vampires (and/or other monsters) join magic-wielding (often leather-clad) heroines to solve mysteries and/or consummate transgressive romances.[2]

The basic component which classifies a narrative of this type is including figures associated explicitly with fantastical conventions, such as (mainly) horror, fantasy and even science fiction among the protagonists and antagonists. The flourishing and multiplication of literary and extra-literary realisations of vampire themes are acknowledged to be the initiation moment for the development of this sub-genre of romance. Still, one of the first works which fell within this subtype is *Sweet Startfire* by Jayne Ann Krentz (part of the *Lost Colony* trilogy), published in 1986.

Love and/or eroticism are central to literature of popular paranormal romance. It is rendered as an emotional relation between a human and a being of supernatural provenance, like a vampire, shape-shifter, ghost, demon, magus, fairy, elf, etc. It also happens that the object of affection is a man endowed with parapsychical powers in the form of telepathy or telekinesis; they can also be time travellers. Researchers trace the roots of the convention to as early as antiquity, pointing to Greek attempts to create the picaresque novel as the most primordial stage of development of the genre; then there were Medieval and early-Renaissance tales called "romances." The formation of distinctive features of the modern paranormal romance was also influenced by the 18th-century sentimental novel, as well as inspirations from the gothic novel, especially with relevant aspects established towards the end of the 18th century and the present-day understanding of "Gothicism," among others, as a category of horror.[3] But as Sam George and Bill Huges suggest romance "inhabitet" by vampire characters is a very interesting problem. They ascerten:

---

[2]   L. M. McLennon, *Defining Urban Fantasy and Paranormal Romance: Crossing Boundaries of Genre, Media, Self and Other in New Supernatural Worlds*, p. 1.

[3]   S. Bruhm, *The Contemporary Gothic: Why We Need It*; E. Cameron *The Psychopathology of the Gothic Romance: Perversion, Neuroses and Psychosis in Early Works of the Genre*.

Since their animation out of folk materials in the nineteenth century by Polidori, as Varney, and in Le Fanu and Stoker, vampires have been continually reborn in modern culture. They have stalked texts from Marx's image of the leeching capitalist, through Pater's Lady Lisa of tainted knowledge, to the multifarious incarnations in contemporary fictions in print and on screen. They have enacted a host of anxieties and desires, shifting shape as the culture they are brought to life in itself changes form. [...] Frayling identified the dominant archetypal vampires as they emerge in fiction: the Byronic vampire (or 'Satanic Lord'), the Fatal Woman, the Unseen Force, the Folkloric Vampire, the 'camp' vampire, and the vampire as creative force. [...] Another strand has since developed – the vampire with a conscience.[4]

McLennos writes also:

Vampire literature in the 1980s and 1990s primarily explores the destabilisation between the boundaries of fantasy and reality, and self and Other, through the trope of the "humanised" or "good" vampire. The figure of the humanised, ethically and spiritually self-conscious vampire first emerged in the late 1970s and early 1980s, in fictions by Fred Saberhagen, Anne Rice, Chelsea Quinn Yarbro, Suzy McKee Charnas, and George R. R. Martin. David Punter and Glennis Byron summarise how the vampire's role in representing the social Other has changed over the last century due to "the modern humanisation of the vampire." They define how "in nineteenth-century fiction, the representation of the vampire as monstrous, evil and other serves to guarantee the existence of good, reinforcing (...) formally dichotomized structures of belief which (...) still constituted the dominant world view." But in vampire fiction in the late twentieth century, the vampire becomes "more sympathetic, closer to the human and much less radically the 'other'" as "the oppositions between good and evil are increasingly problematized."

The vampires and other "humanised" monsters of UF/PR develop from this earlier trend begun in the vampire literature of the 1970s. UF/PR in the 1980s and 1990s likewise destabilises the assumed connections between monstrosity, evil and Otherness. For example, vampires like Killough's Garreth Mikaelian, Huff's Henry Fitzroy and *Forever Knight's* Nicholas

---

4 S. George, B. Hughes, *Introduction: Undead Reflections The Sympathetic Vampire and its Monstrous Other*, pp. 1-3.

Knight struggle against their monstrous ontologies in order to be "good people." Many of these protagonists face torturous ethical struggles similar to those of Anne Rice's well-known vampire aesthetes in *Interview with the Vampire* (...) Vampires in 1990s urban fantasy differ on one important point: to be good vampires, they must *refuse* to drink human blood. Through their determined abstinence, the vampires of these early urban fantasy texts become the first truly "good" vampires in fiction, television and film. For the first time, vampire fiction in the 1990s broadly explored the concept of vampires who want to do and be good in the human world by acting as human as possible. Throughout this decade, the convention of the abstaining vampire remained popular.[5]

The fiction-related schemes of paranormal romances are, as a rule, very similar to one another. According to Eva Illouz (comparing romantic love to an economic system) writes:

> In romantic love, [...] two individuals are bound together by the "capacity to realism spontaneity and empathy in an erotic relationship." In the marketplace, trading partners are ultimately interchangeable; relationships shift with economic circumstances. In romantic love, the person we love and feel united with is unique and irreplaceable; furthermore, "love is the most important thing in the world, to which all other considerations, particularly material ones, should be sacrificed." Romantic love is irrational rather than rational, gratuitous rather than profit-oriented, organic rather than utilitarian, private rather than public.[6]

Although the authors' predilection for reorganising the paradigm of traditional romance forges a clear compositional dominant, while a significant element is also to twist conventions by reinterpreting well-known constructional systems, the main backbone of fiction remains intact. Scenes of accidental meetings are obligatory (some are entangled in heroic deeds resulting inthe glorification of the adorer or the heroine), along with infatuation, incidental or intentional deepening of the acquaintance, hesitation between hostility and desire, sometimes a realisation of erotic needs, quarrel/conflict/misunderstanding/parting,

---

[5] L. M. McLennon, op. cit., pp. 8-9.
[6] E. Illouz, *Consuming the Romantic Utopia. Love and the Cultural Contradictions of Capitalism*, p. 2.

and finally – a love happy ending. In the paranormal variant, sequences appear connected with the partner's adjustment to functioning in a liminal world. Such a situation occurs particularly in plots where the dichotomy of the world corresponds to the typology put forward by Farah Mendlesohn as liminal fantasy. The researcher writes:

> Liminal fantasy (…) was *that form of fantasy which estranges the reader from the fantastic as seen and described by the protagonist* (…). The liminal fantasy can be balanced between or […] it can be truly liminal, "what it's like to have fallen into the crack." However, rather than being (…) "anti-structural" this fiction is striking for just how tightly structured it is. (…) Crucial to the structure of liminal fantasy is that it is a two-way process. It depends on *knowingness*, or what Barthes described as a shared code (…). Although the dialectic between reader and author is always central to the *construction* of the fantastic. (…) The construction of the category *liminal* fantasy builds on Jameson's argument that genres are social contracts "between a writer and a specific public." (…) The difficulty with this form of fantasy, however, was that it had no obvious boundaries. It seemed to come into the classic category of "I know it when I see it."[7]

The supernatural element is found in the area of the protagonists' cognitive peripheries: hidden and inaccessible to the unauthorised, not revealing its existence explicitly. The essence of the beings that function therein is defined with reference to the context of extra-fantastic reality, as Mendlesohn points out: "to subvert the immersion is that in some way or other, the fantastic within the text should be as alien to the protagonist as it is to us."[8] In order to enter the liminal world, it is necessary to work out a form of transition between the worlds – and in the case of paranormal romance this is neither a portal nor a gate, since the border between the worlds is of a more conventional nature and its area is marked out, in a sense, by the discretion of people and beings who travel between them. It is they who decide whether or not to keep the secret, understanding that their world and the world of humans cannot coexist in a safe manner. Farah Medlesohn, while writing about the impression that this secrecy regarding fantasy elements evokes, says that it interfaces with the sense that the reader knows what is fantasy and realises

[7]   F. Mendlesohn, *Rhetorics of Fantasy*, loc. 4024–4052.
[8]   Ibidem, loc. 4215.

at which moment one enters this liminal world.[9] The fantasy element revealed before the eyes of the hero, who crosses the threshold of the worlds, is neither destructive to his psyche nor does it provoke extreme emotions, but – as Mendlesohn sees it – it does to some extent draw away the reader, for whom the bi-world exists more clearly than for the protagonist and from this point of view it is possible to more distinctly perceive the demarcation line between the two.

The paranormal romance places beings associated directly with figures of menace and horror – vampires, werewolves, demons, or even zombies – in the role of the adorer (and often in that of the heroine). The beasts to date, despite the fact that they represent non-human elements and that their psychological profiles (especially in the initial sequences) fairly frequently depart from the ideal model of an object of affection, go through a metamorphosis under the influence of feelings and reveal their truer, better natures. This particular betterment of figures unambiguously identified with the realm of horror goes in line with the discourse of taming the strangeness by means of trans-fictional mechanisms (in the understanding of Richard Saint-Gelais and Marie-Laure Ryan).[10] Making use of figures or characters known from fairy tales, folklore, mythology or literature testifies not only to the need for modernising or – at least – retelling, but directly to predilections towards constructing new or alternative biographies for them in the context of themes of a romance nature. It is also linked with McLennon's conclusion related to the issue of Otherness and monstrosity:

> In the everyday-supernatural world, monster hunters and slayers lose their moral certainty as protagonists, further destabilising the binaries of real/fantastic, human/Other and good/evil. As Graham writes, "One of the ways in particular in which the boundaries between humans and

[9]   Ibidem, loc. 4224.
[10] According to Ryan, transfictionality "refers to the migration of fictional entities cross different texts, but these texts may belong to the same medium, usually written narrative fiction. Transmedial storytelling can be regarded as a special case of transfictionality – a transfictionality that operates across many different media" (see M.-L. Ryan, *Transmedial Storytelling and Transfictionality*, p. 366). Richard Saint-Gelais maintained that: "Two (or more) texts exhibit a transfictional relation when they share elements such as characters, imaginary locations, or fictional worlds. Transfictionality may be considered a branch of intertextuality, but it usually conceals this intertextual link because it neither quotes nor acknowledges its sources. Instead, it uses the source text's setting and/or inhabitants as if they existed independently" (R. Saint-Gelais, *Transficionality*, p. 612).

almost-humans have been asserted is through the discourse of 'monstrosity.' Monsters serve both to mark the fault-lines but also, subversively, to signal the fragility of such boundaries." In texts which use everyday-supernatural settings, humans and monsters must constantly renegotiate the boundaries between self and Other in order to co-exist successfully. In these fictional worlds, heroines are no longer able to uphold human law and protect the innocent, because human law can no longer adequately account for cultural and ethical differences between the monstrous and the human inhabitants of society.[11]

Aformentioned "Otherness" have been present in classical romance genre, as Kimberly A. Frohreich says:

> The traditional vampire has always threatened binaries, such as dead/alive, animal/human, male/ female, heterosexual/homosexual, and has often functioned as a destabiliser of the category of race. Donna Haraway writes, "for better and for worse, vampires are vectors of category transformation in a racialised, historical, national unconscious." The vampire is "a figure that both promises and threatens racial and sexual mixing." Bram Stoker's Dracula miscegenates – he mixes blood with white English women and uses their bodies to 'reproduce' other vampires. However, this practice is part of what makes him 'threatening' and 'monstrous,' contributing to his characterisation as the ethnic and/or racial Other. Indeed, Stoker's novel illustrates Western European anxieties regarding Eastern European immigrants and the potential loss of supposed racial and/or ethnic purity. (…) So while it can be said that the traditional vampire destabilises racial boundaries, the figure has also player into stigmatising definitions of the racial Other in relation to white normativity.[12]

But "contemporary vampire fiction recycles early fictional tropes and consciously incorporates the scientific and legal discourses as well as the social practices that have surrounded the cultural construction of race, questioning the link between the racial Other and the monstrous Other."[13]

---

[11]   L. M. McLennon, op. cit., p. 5.
[12]   K. A. Frohreich, *Sullied Blood, Semen and Skin Vampires and the Spectre of Miscegenation*, pp. 33-34.
[13]   Ibidem, p. 35.

Contemporary vampire characters seems to become rather different; especially in paranormal romance: despite everything, the adorers' distinctive features do not undergo any basic modifications. Attractive men, physically fit, strong, possessing material wealth, sometimes also a high social position or, at least, prospects of attaining one, still remain objects of affection. Assets of character are also written into the poetics of the romance, determining psychic stability, generosity, loyalty, faithfulness, pride or courage. The features typical of the 20th and 21st-century romance, such as casting chiefs, leaders, millionaires, owners of corporations and even aristocrats into the role of heroes also occur in forms of supernatural provenance, which is significant in the context of the Marxist interpretation of vampirism, raised by Franco Moretti (1982) or indicated by Emily S. Davis.[14]

The specificity of paranormal romance results from a resignation from typically strictly love-oriented themes in favour of fantasy and a world-creative element. Many writings that belong to this sub-type become extensive series taking place in *universa* which are constructed in every detail. It is possible to notice this tendency in three series of vampire novels, which will serve as exemplifications: *Love at Stake* by Kerrelyn Sparks, *Guardians of Eternity* by Alexanry Ivy[15] or *Midnight Breed* by Lary Adrian.

The significant correlation between vampirism and eroticism is a sum of multifarious factors, among which the leading motif is the predilection for imbuing acts of blood-sucking with explicitly sexual connotations, the inclination acquiring a firmer and firmer presence in the literary tradition.

> Some hidden aspects of sexual pathology are lurking in vampires as well. Fetishism, sadism, masochism, and homosexuality were sub-divisions of *paraesthesia* for Krafft-Ebing. Fetishism is using with sexual connotation as a substitute for the sexual object. It can be a piece of clothing or any anatomical part(s) of the partner. Freud calls the fetish "a substitute for the penis" (*Fetishism* 953). In the case of vampires the substitute element is blood. Blood becomes the exclusive object of sexuality. Haematophilia and haemotodipsia are under the class of blood fetishism.

[14]   E. S. Davis, *Rethinking the Romance Genre. Global Intimacies in Contemporary Literary and Visual Culture.*
[15]   Properly: Debbie (Deborah) Raleigh.

The haematophiliac has an erotic attraction to the taste, sight or smell of blood. Haemotodipsia is a stronger form of this disease. People gain their whole sexual satisfaction from blood, that is "what coitus is to the lover, the bite and the sucking is to the haemotodipsiac" […]. Blood and lust pervade the legends of Vlad Țepeș, Elizabeth Bathory and Stoker's Dracula. Sexual sadism, this psychosexual disorder links these stories, where mutilation of the body is connected with delight and pleasure. Burning, boiling, beating and several other brutal and tantalizing tortures have become essential parts of the popularized image about the life style of these "vampirized" historical persons. Functionally, these sadistic elements satisfy all demands of people's insatiable appetite for dread and horror in the given era.[16]

In an opposite interpretation, contemporary vampire becomes the embodiment of an ideal lover, since they have at their disposal a whole spectrum of attributes which are inaccessible to an ordinary male. For example – as Sam George and Bill Hughes say – "the sympathetic vampire rules."[17] It is very clear that in paranormal romance almost all supernatural characters are modelled in compliance with a similar psychological pattern, constituting a set of features that determine an asocial, introverted individual rather than a sentimental adorer, sensitive, caring, deeply engaged in building a relationship. Here, one example are the very old vampires from the Sparks series, warriors of the Order from the Adrian collection, or nearly all the characters of this kind in Ivy's novels. Each time, longevity and boredom with emotional aspects of existence come to be an interpretation of asocial behaviour and a desire for isolation. Freeing oneself from carnal and feeling-related desires equals self-control consisting in retreat from any closer interactions, especially ones with the opposite sex. An unchanging element is therefore a rather long period of celibacy, exposed every time as the story of the character is narrated. Sexual restraint plays a dual role here: firstly – the protagonists' erotic inclinations are directed at specific women and become a proof of the highest degree of devotion to their chosen ones; secondly, in a sense they "guarantee" a *happy ending* (thus the supposition of faithfulness), which is possible only when there are no doubts as to heroes'

[16]   E. Muskovits, *The Threat of Otherness in Bram Stoker's Dracula*, p. 4.
[17]   S. George, B. Hughes, op. cit., p. 5.

emotional intentions.[18] Bodily cleanliness – standing in stark opposition to subsequent eruption of desires – is an immanent component certifying the purity of the man's intentions, who – indeed – exclusively wants a woman who will win his affections.

As a rule, breaking the given schema of vampires' misogynous behavior takes place in a very simple way, that is by attributing characteristics satisfying the exorbitant requirements of supernatural adorers to eventually chosen women (*Love at Stake* by Sparks) or also their possession of genetic conditions which evoke the fascination of beings of supernatural provenance, uncompromising in principle (*Midnight Breed* by Adrian, *Guardians of Eternity* by Ivy). The elimination of emotional resistance takes place unexpectedly after all, sometimes against the will and wishes of protagonists of either sex. Initially, the factor which determines emotional behavior is lust, oriented at a specific object and continued in the form of a drive for physical fulfillment, most often as the consequence of a satisfying coincidence. With time (very shortly as a rule) the loose relation of an exclusively sexual nature transforms into a deep affection which both lovers must accept, resisting it to a lesser or greater extent to finally attain satisfaction in love. Obviously, the element of disavowal is here constitutive for the later spectacular and final declaration or display of love. It is clear then that sexual fascinations are finally implied by forces which are independent from the protagonists. These forces can be called destiny or a disposition of Providence, the model being most clearly executed by Ivy who consistently invests the vampires' beloved with attributes of a supernatural nature and – at the same time – ascertaining that such strong relationships are possible solely in the perspective of fate designated to individuals (the case of Anna, being the Oracle [*Darkness Revealed*] or Leylah, called *principium* due to herprophesied momentous role in the order of the world [*Devoured by Darkness*]).

Love seems to be an affectation that poses a threat to a man's own identity, formed arduously and not constituted by nature – as has happened to date – which explains the protagonists' difficulty in reconciling

[18]   In as much as in Sparks's series love is each time concluded in nuptials (which in itself does not guarantee faithfulness), in the Adrian's and Ivy's series, partnership with a vampire materialises through the ritual of drinking blood together, following which a betrayal is simply not possible. Vampires and their chosen ones lose interest in other individuals, since the bond between them is so firm that the need for erotic encounters with anyone but their beloved disappears completely.

with the assumed role of an individual who is deeply in love. The realisation of this fact by the hero is simultaneously a test of strength (coming to grips with himself) and an endeavour to redefine himself in the context of newly-discovered emotionality. Vampiric lovers, succumbing to carnal temptation, do not realise the implication of getting closer to a woman, whose very presence evokes desires and needs thus far unknown. In this way, the creators of paranormal romances mark the extraordinariness of supernatural-human relationships, explicating their exceptionality through hyperbolising the ecstatic illumination of the vampiric protagonist towards the feeling of love.

Here, it is worth paying attention to the fact that the majority, if not all vampiric heroes are warriors, deeply believing in the rightness of their crusade against evil. This immersion in the belligerent amok does not relent until the appearance of a suitable partner who initially introduces an element of dispersion, then leads to a change in priorities (as takes place in the majority of novels in the series by Sparks, as well as those by Adrian and Ivy). Such a system is slightly reminiscent of a fairy-tale-like removal of a charm or illusion, in which the hero was submerged. In this case, the emergence of the chosen one – as the one and only – determines a liberation from the imperatives to date. This move also provides a peculiar *catharsis* in relation to the past negative or traumatic experience with which the protagonist had not been able to cope thus far or which he had ousted from his consciousness.

The social role of man underwent, especially at the turn of the 20th and the 21st century, considerable revaluation, hence the supposition that the presence of a vampire in paranormal romance constitutes not only a result of associating this being with eroticism or – simply – with a vogue for this literary figure, but also connects somehow with secret needs of contemporary women. It is well-known that vampires, as long-living beings (and there are a great number of heroes exceeding the age of 100 years in this type of literary production), represent values which are presently superseded, irrelevant or that symbolise a negated past. However, they doubtlessly function in female readers' imaginations as strong, uncompromising, brave, slightly aggressive or predatory individuals with deeply rooted moral principles. At the same time, the representation (perchance resulting from a longing for a given type of male) formed by the knight's ethos about the respect for women and its prime position in relations with them is also vital. Such needs are explicated literally or through sexual fantasies conceived by heroines of paranormal romances. In this dimension, the vampire functions as an almost ideal creation, thus contaminating all the attributes characteristic of a perfect lover: brutality directed at enemies, subtlety and sensitivity reserved for the chosen one, decidedness and determination both in fighting foes and winning woman's favours, sentimentality, yet ruthlessness or the lack of inhibitions while confronted with danger. The traits of a vampire-lover include the embodiment of women's representations about an ideal partner – both in physical and psychological dimensions; nevertheless, the dark secret (kept hidden by each heroup to a point) eventually constitutes a form of aphrodisiac which makes relationships additionally attractive.

At the same time, the vampire in a paranormal romance embodies "soft" emotions and "macho"-like behavioural patterns and the blend results in an almost spectacular expertise in the art of love. Satisfying a partner's needs is the supreme principle behind intercourse, the relevant drive being underlined with full narrative force as well as in the internal monologues of the vampiric lovers. The above can be illustrated with the following quotes:

He glanced at her, his hair wild and his eyes red. "May I give ye pleasure?"[19]

He skimmed along the slick folds, then gently parted them. He dipped a finger inside and stroked the inner walls. *Do you like that? Or do you prefer this?* He circled her clitoris, then teased the tip. She cried out. She twisted the sheet in her hands. She longed to hold him, run her hands through his hair, feel the muscles on his back and buttocks. This was so one-sided. But so damned good. He inserted two fingers inside her. At least, she thought it was two fingers. Maybe three. Oh God, he was torturing her from the inside out. His fingers circled and stroked, plunged and withdrew. She had no idea how many thousands of nerve endings she possessed down there, but he seemed determined to set each one on fire. He rubbed the hard, swollen nub of her sex faster and faster. She dug her heels into the mattress, tensing her legs and pressing her hips into the air. *More. More.* He gave her more.[20]

[19]   K. Sparks, *Be Still My Vampire Heart*, p. 160.
[20]   Eadem, *How to Marry a Millionaire Vampire*, p. 183.

She came swiftly, harder than she could have imagined. Lucan held her firmly in his hands, pressing her damp core to him, giving no quarter as her body quivered and bucked, her breath falling to a strangled gasp as he stroked her toward the crest of another climax.[21]

–I was greedy, he murmured, bending down to kiss her in apology. He didn't dare get close to her luscious throat, not when his fangs were throbbing with another need that was raging to be sated. –If you want, we can take it slower now. –Don't you dare, she said, wrapping her legs around his thighs to make her point. (…) Elise's climax was swiftly building too. She took him deeper with every furious pound of their meeting flesh, clutching at his shoulders and panting as her body's need overtook her. Tegan could feel her pleasure in each stroke of his fingers on her flesh, each silken caress of her core. Her emotion seeped into him from every point of contact, swamping him with a surfeit of sensation. He absorbed everything she gave him, all his focus on bringing her toward a shattering release.[22]

His hips rocked faster, his hands tilting her hips upward to meet his deep, steady thrusts. "Jagr…please," she muttered against his lips, her body clenched so tightly she felt as if she might shatter. "Patience, little one." Dipping his head downward, he teased her aching nipple with his lips and fangs, his hips pumping faster and faster as she arched off the bed to meet him. Regan's breath rasped in the silent air, her world narrowing to the point where Jagr's body surged in and out of her. She was so close. So exquisitely close. And then…it happened. With one last surge he tumbled her over the edge, sending her into a vortex of dizzying bliss. He swallowed her scream of pleasure with a searing kiss.[23]

Undoubtedly, what catches our attention is that each time vampiric adorers are portrayed in compliance with popular beliefs relating to female fantasies about men who represent a set of determined external features, such as being well-built and muscular, arrestingly handsome or generously endowed (this being as essential in paranormal romance designed for adults as in professional pornographic movie productions). In this drive towards creating an ideal partner, the objectification

[21] L. Adrian, *Kiss of Crimson*, p. 99.
[22] Eadem, *Veil of Midnight*, pp. 213-214
[23] Eadem, *Shades of Midnight*, p. 104.

of a man's body is clearly seen: it becomes invested exclusively with values serving the purpose of giving pleasure – aesthetic as well as erotic. The male is perceived here through the prism of attractiveness, which is confirmed by numerous passages relating to the visual impressions of women-characters:

There he was on the far side of the king-sized bed, lying on top of a tan suede comforter. His face was turned away from her, so all she could see was his thick black hair and the ponytail that curled on top of the pillow. Some men might look effeminate with shoulder-length hair and a skirt, but on Ian, the effect was quite the opposite. There was something wild and rugged about him, like a Scottish warrior who refused to be civilized. Just the sight of him made her heartbeat quicken and thoughts of rebellion sneak into her head. (…) The thick black fringe of his eyelashes cast a shadow on his pale cheeks. Beautiful. A man shouldn't look that sweet and rugged at the same time.[24]

Every cell in her body was aware of this man. Was it her imagination, or were his eyes growing more golden, more intense? His shoulder-length black hair curled slightly on the ends. A black sweater accentuated broad shoulders, and black jeans hugged his hips and long legs. He was a tall, dark, and handsome…[25]

Good Lord, this guy was sexy. And much too gorgeous for his own good. No doubt he had trouble finding clothes that fit those broad shoulders and long legs. He probably had problems with women, too. They took one look at him and their clothes accidentally fell off.[26]

Spiky black hair falling loosely around a broad, intelligent brow and lean, angular cheeks. A strong, stern jaw. And his mouth … his mouth was generous and sensual, even when quirked in that cynical, almost cruel line.[27]

Elise had seen his impressive Breed skin markings once before, when she'd first spoken with him at the Order's compound a few months ago.

[24] K. Sparks, *All I Want for Christmas Is a Vampire*, pp. 38–41.
[25] Eadem, *How to Marry a Millionaire Vampire*, p. 14.
[26] Eadem, *All I Want for Christmas Is a Vampire*, p. 14.
[27] L. Adrian, *Kiss of Crimson*, p. 12.

She didn't want to stare, but it was hard not to marvel at the swirling arcs and elegant, interlocking geometric designs that distinguished Tegan as one of the oldest of the race. He was of the Breed's first generation; if the depth of his powers didn't out him as such, the prevalence and complexity of his *glyphs* certainly did.[28]

Okay, the damned vamp was the most beautiful creature she'd ever seen. And he oozed sex from the top of his golden head to the tips of his shit-kicker boots.[29]

The liking of heroines, and by supposition – also female readers – for a specific type of masculine good looks and behaviour results from the fact that much of the mass media forms a very precise picture of masculine appearance, character and demeanour, and the elements which constitute it are as follows: success, professional activity, physical and intellectual attractiveness and the satisfying of erotic relations. In the case of vampires featuring in novels, all of the above-mentioned attributes find their application with reference to almost each hero. In Sparks's series, the head of Romatech, vampire Roman Draganesti, and his collaborators, be they security guards, scientists or accountants, are all professionally and financially fulfilled. As far as Adrian's novels are concerned, vampires form very egalitarian units and the Order are composed of model examples of self-realisation. In the case of Ivy's creations, the principle of the ideal of man is applicable in descriptions of the majority of male protagonists, with few exceptions when it comes to the state of possession or social position. However, even if for some reason the protagonist does not have any one of the material assets at their disposal, they acquire so in the course of narration, some examples of which may be Phinneas the vampire (from Sparks's series) who was young and brought up in a poor family, Sterling Chase (from Adrian's novel) – lacking a professional position – or the alienated Styx (from Ivy's series). A satisfying erotic life, in turn, does not come their way until they meet their dreamt of chosen one. This is then when the sexual relation is depicted as the most sanctified and – because of this – enhancing the fulfilment.

---

[28]   Eadem, *Veil of Midnight*, p. 62.
[29]   A. Ivy, *Darkness Unleashed*, p. 49.

It is worth paying attention to the sociological aspect, and thus the context in which metaphysical romances (or romances in general) are created, since they become a realisation of universal imaginations and these – in turn – constitute the interpretation of a determined image of a hero in similar literature. Each time, however, the vampires featured in novels reflect distinctive features of an ideal male, promoted, as it was mentioned earlier, by various media.

Sexualia are located within this field, too. They – similarly to other elements of the ideal model – are subjected to qualitative stereotyping. By offering protagonists, who are as attractive as erotically fit, to female recipients the authors involve the latter in building representations of a perfect relationship, in which mutual satisfaction is a *conditiosine qua non*. Sexual acts in paranormal romances (very often a prelude to a lasting relationship) are indeed of a pornographic nature and their descriptions can be very literal, not to say – balancing on the bounds of good taste. Nevertheless, the element that they always have in common is admiration for his or her partner's body, with descriptions containing – as a rule – adjectives which valorise the object of desire. This is the case, for example, in Sparks's novel *Sexiest Vampire Alive*, when the heroine, overwhelmed with desire, looks at her lover and concludes in her thoughts that Gregori was the sexiest man she had seen in her life. A similar model can be observed in Adrian's and Ivy's novels, an exemplification of which are the following fragments:

> Her gaze fell to the dimple in his chin. It had been one of the first things she'd noticed about him. The whole time he'd been fussing at her, she'd wanted to poke it with her finger. She reached out her hand, then snatched it back. What was she thinking? He was one of them.[30]

> Ian had forgotten how pretty she was – pretty enough to scramble his thoughts for a second. But it didn't matter how shiny and golden her hair was, or how pink and sweetly curved her mouth was.[31]

[30]   K. Sparks, *All I Want for Christmas Is a Vampire*, p. 41.
[31]   Ibidem, p. 49.

His back was to her. Wisps of clouds floated past him, stirring his kilt. Moonlight gleamed off his dark red hair. Mist swirled around him, making him look ethereal. Like the ghost of a Highland warrior.[32]

Her heart ached in her chest. Oh God, he was everything she'd ever wanted in a man.[33]

He smiled. Damn, he was too good-looking for a demon.[34]

He was soaking wet and naked from the waist up, wearing only loose-fitting gray cotton sweats that looked like they'd been yanked on just seconds before. His dark head hung low, long espresso-brown waves sleek with water and drooping over his face. The *dermaglyphs* that tracked up his bare chest and over his shoulders were livid with color, the intricate pattern of Breed skin markings pulsing with furious life.[35]

Despite his cool demeanor, color had risen in his Gen One *dermaglyphs*. The beautiful markings had swirled like elaborate, changeable tattoos across Tegan's muscular chest, arms, and torso…and down, beneath the tight black swimsuit that blatantly accentuated his profane sexuality.[36]

Idealising lovers' bodies translates into their sexual effectiveness and the ability to experience ecstasy many times, also closely linkedwith the peculiar fetishisation of simultaneous orgasms. In the popular belief, one condition of satisfying intercourse is the simultaneous experiencing of sexual fulfilment by both partners; therefore, in paranormal romances, each coitus is not only satisfying to the partners, but this very satisfaction takes place each time at the same moment. This is testified to by absolutely all the descriptions of sexual acts found in the above-mentioned series of novels.

Also, a vital component of female-and-male intimacies are the erotic allusions which abound in the protagonists' conversations. They form a prolog to a carnal relationship. A similar role is played by sexual

[32]   Eadem, *Be Still My Vampire Heart*, p. 21.
[33]   Ibidem, p. 145.
[34]   Eadem, *How to Marry a Millionaire Vampire*, p. 136.
[35]   L. Adrian, *Kiss of Crimson*, p. 35.
[36]   Eadem, *Veil of Midnight*, p. 115.

imagining, which only one of the parties – as a rule – is engaged in; the subsequent sexual act merely complements it. The object of erotic imagining typically realises that the interest is of a fantasising nature, which in itself creates a strong sexual impulse. Thus, there forms a bond between the protagonists, which they do not want to mention at first; nevertheless, under the influence of circumstances, their mutual relations develop from fantasising, through a sexual intercourse, only to end in an affection and a lasting relationship.

The instances of the metaphysical romances series by Adrian, Ivy and Sparks point to a clear predilection towards changing the optics while creating a vampire-lover. The vampire, representing multifaceted monstrosity symptomatically transforms into an adorer, an object of desire, fascination and an element of erotic *imaginarium*. The archetypical bloodsucker is no longer a mere perpetrator of atrocities but has acquired characteristics that identify him unambiguously as an adorer. In this narrative, traditional methods of presenting vampirism recede into the background and are replaced by ones which are less readily associated with horror and more with romance. Although it is true that the most stereotypical representations become assimilated in the novels (in a milder form, though, like for instance, feeding on exclusively synthetic blood in Spark's or Ivy's novels), making them comply with the romance convention brings out, first of all, aspects connected with sexuality. In a similar framework, vampires are shown as super-lovers, whose erotic potential is far superior to that of humans and whose sensuality and, simultaneously, sensitivity to women's needs (including emotional ones), determines their perception as ideal models.

The inspiration with eroticism entangled in what is not completely dead has turned out to be a successful move – even more so in terms of the profitability of an extensive readership that prefers metaphysical romance. Elements of the aesthetics of horror combined with one of the most popular genres of novel have become a hallmark of a great number of series devoted to these motifs. A side effect of this drive, on the other hand, has been the new meaning bestowed upon the vampire, determined by aesthetic requirements, as well as a significant reduction of the vampire to sexuality and aspects related to it.

Adrian L., *Kiss of Crimson*, Dell Pub Co., New York 2007a.

Adrian L., *Kiss of Midnight*, Robinson, London 2007b.

Adrian L., *Midnight Awakening*, Dell Pub Co., New York 2007c.

Adrian L., *Midnight Rising*, Dell Pub Co., New York 2008a.

Adrian L., *Veil of Midnight*, Dell Pub Co., New York 2008b.

Adrian L., *Ashes of Midnight*, Dell Pub Co., New York 2009a.

Adrian L., *Shades of Midnight*, New York: Dell Pub Co., New York 2009b.

Adrian L., *Taken by Midnight*, Dell Pub Co., New York 2010.

Adrian L., *Deeper than Midnight*, Dell Pub Co., New York 2011.

Adrian L., *Darker after Midnight*, Dell Pub Co., New York 2012.

Adrian L., *Edge of Dawn*, Dell Pub Co., New York 2013.

Adrian L., *Crave the Night*, Dell Pub Co., New York 2014.

Adrian L., *Bound to Darkness*, Dell Pub Co., New York 2015.

Bruhm S., *The Contemporary Gothic: Why We Need It* [in:] *The Cambridge Companion to Gothic Fiction*, Cambridge University Press, Cambridge 2002.

Cameron E., *The Psychopathology of the Gothic Romance: Perversion, Neuroses and Psychosis in Early Works of the Genre*, McFarland & Co, Jefferson 2010.

Davis E. S., *Rethinking the Romance Genre. Global Intimacies in Contemporary Literary and Visual Culture*, Palgrave Macmilan, New York 2013.

Frohreich K. A., *Sullied Blood, Semen and Skin Vampires and the Spectre of Miscegenation*, "Gothic Studies", No. 1, 2013.

Frye N., *The Secular Scripture: A Study of the Structure of Romance*, Harvard University Press, Cambridge 1978.

George S., Hughes B., *Introduction: Undead Reflections. The Sympathetic Vampire and its Monstrous Other*, "Gothic Studies", No. 1, 2013.

Illouz E., *Consuming the Romantic Utopia. Love and the Cultural Contradictions of Capitalism*, California University Press, Berkeley 2008.

Ivy A., *Embrace the Darkness*, Zebra Books, New York 2007a.

Ivy A., *When Darkness Comes*, Zebra Books, New York 2007b.

Ivy A., *Darkness Everlasting*, Zebra Books, New York 2008.

Ivy A., *Darkness Revealed*, Zebra Books, New York 2009a.

Ivy A., *Darkness Unleashed*, Zebra Books, New York 2009b.

Ivy A., *Beyond the Darkness*, Zebra Books, New York 2010a.

Ivy A., *Devoured by Darkness*, Zebra Books, New York 2010b.

Ivy A., *Bound by Darkness*, Zebra Books, New York 2011.

Ivy A., *Fear the Darkness*, Zebra Books, New York 2012.

Ivy A., *Darkness Avenged*, Zebra Books, New York 2013.

Ivy A., *Hunt the Darkness*, Zebra Books, New York 2014.

Ivy A., *When Darkness Ends*, Zebra Books, New York 2015.

McLennon L. M., *Defining Urban Fantasy and Paranormal Romance: Crossing Boundaries of Genre, Media, Self and Other in New Supernatural Worlds*, "Refractory: A Journal of Entertainment Media", Vol. 23, 2014.

Mendlesohn F., *Rhetorics of Fantasy*, Wesleyan University Press, Middletown 2008, Kindle edition.

Muskovits E., *The Threat of Otherness in Bram Stoker's Dracula*, "Trans", No. 10, 2010.

Radway J. A., *Reading the Romance. Women, Patriarchy and Popular Literature*, University of North Carolina Press, Chapel Hill 1991.

Ryan M.-L., *Transmedial Storytelling and Transfictionality*, "Poetics Today", No. 3, 2013.

Saint-Gelais R., *Contours de la transfictionnalité* [in:] *La fiction, suites et variations*, R. Audet, R. Saint-Gelais (eds.), Editions Nota Bene, Québec 2007.

Saint-Gelais R., *Transficionality* [in:] *Routledge Encyclopedia of Narrative Theory*, D. Herman, M. Jahm, M.-L. Ryan (eds.), Routledge, London–New York 2008.

Sparks K., *How to Marry a Millionaire Vampire*, Harper Collins, New York 2005.

Sparks K., *Vamps and the City*, Harper Collins, New York 2006.

Sparks K., *Be Still My Vampire Heart*, Harper Collins, New York 2007.

Sparks K., *All I Want for Christmas Is a Vampire*, Harper Collins, New York 2008a.

Sparks K., *The Undead Next Door*, Harper Collins, New York 2008b.

Sparks K., *Forbidden Nights with a Vampire*, Harper Collins, New York 2009a.

Sparks K., *Secret Life of a Vampire*, Harper Collins, New York 2009b.

Sparks K., *Eat Prey Love*, Harper Collins, New York 2010.

Sparks K., *Sexiest Vampire Alive*, Harper Collins, New York 2011a.

Sparks K., *Vampire Mine*, Harper Collins, New York 2011b.

Sparks K., *Wanted: Undead or Alive*, Harper Collins, New York 2012a.

Sparks K., *Wild about You*, Harper Collins, New York 2012b.

Sparks K., *The Vampire with the Dragon Tattoo*, Harper Collins, New York 2013.

Sparks K., *Crouching Tiger, Forbidden Vampire*, Harper Collins, New York 2014a.

Sparks K., *How to Seduce a Vampire (without Really Trying)*, Harper Collins, New York 2014b.

JOANNA MALITA-KRÓL
http://orcid.org/0000-0002-7668-5902

THE HORNED GOD: DIVINE MALE PRINCIPLE IN BRITISH TRADITIONAL WICCA

Abstract: The duotheistic approach to divinity has been visible in British Traditional Wicca since its inception – that is, worshipping two complementary principles, female and male, a passive and fertile Goddess alongside an active and fertilising God. The aim of this paper is to provide an insight into the God in his four aspects: mainly the Horned One, but also Lord of Death, Oak and Holly King, Green Man. Basing on sources written by Traditional Wiccans, the contributors to the development of the religion (among them, Gerald Gardner, Doreen Valiente and the Farrars), the God is characterised as full of strength, vigour and sexuality, the one who fertilises the land, ruler of woodland and patron of animals. Events of his life, celebrated during the Wheel of the Year's festivals, reflect the journey of the Sun during the astronomical year. The God remains equal in importance to the Goddess, as they are both necessary for the world to maintain balance.

Keywords: witchcraft, British Traditional Wicca, Wicca, Pagan studies, Horned God

> *By the flame that burneth bright,*
> *O Horned One!*
> *We call thy name into the night,*
> *O Ancient One!*
>
> Invocation of the Horned God
> by Doreen Valiente[1]

---

[1]   D. Valiente, *Witchcraft for Tomorrow*, p. 190.

Modern Pagan witchcraft in its abundance of traditions, paths and currents reveres numerous forms of deities, perceived as Jungian archetypes, actual beings, forms of energy, symbols etc. Some would adhere to the conviction that "all the gods are one god, and all the goddesses are one goddess, and there is one initiator,"[2] acknowledging deities from different pantheons and cultures as representing one ultimate, divine pair: the Goddess and the God. This duotheistic vision echoes very clearly in British Traditional Wicca, which is sometimes called the religion of modern witches. Rising from the British occultist milieu in the mid twentieth century, Wicca – referred to in the 1950s and 1960s mainly as simply "witchcraft" or "the Craft" – was first introduced in 1954 as the survival of an ancient, pre-Christian witch cult. Thanks to the activity and works of Gerald B. Gardner it has gained more and more followers and started to be spread, reinterpreted and adopted all over the world. Gardnerian (originating from Gardner himself) and Alexandrian (named after Alex Sanders) traditions have been formed, and other movements inspired by Wicca have appeared, drawing from, among others, counter-culture, feminism, and ecology.[3] From mystery cult to Goddess-centred nature religion, today's Wicca is a broad movement, embracing different beliefs, praxes and worldviews from Australia to the United States. British Traditional Wicca, however, is limited to two traditions: Gardnerian and Alexandrian,[4] and only someone initiated in a coven within one of these traditions is acknowledged as a Traditional Wiccan.[5]

What matters most in the context of this article, in Wicca no official authority nor dogma is established, which can be perceived as its forte and weak point at the same time. Consequently, different traditions, gatherings, covens or individuals may have developed their own visions of the divine. Even in British Traditional Wicca, wherein a certain content is handed down within the initiation line, it is the practice that matters

[2] Famous phrase coined by Dion Fortune in her *The Sea Priestess*, p. 172.
[3] On the history of Wicca, see for example R. Hutton, *The Triumph of the Moon*; P. Heselton, *Wiccan Roots: Gerald Gardner and the Modern Witchcraft Revival*; E. Doyle White, *Wicca. History, Belief and Community in Modern Pagan Witchcraft*.
[4] On the distinction between those traditions see E. Doyle White, op. cit., pp. 41ff; V. Crowley, *Wicca. A Comprehensive Guide to the Old Religion in the Modern World*, pp. 35-36. Crowley herself has been initiated to both traditions and joins them in her own practice, and so the line started by her is sometimes perceived as a third, "mixed" tradition.
[5] Coven is a gathering of witches, which meet regularly to celebrate, conduct rituals, practice magic and also teach newcomers. The actual term is used both in British Traditional Wicca and other, more eclectic paths.

the most, not the individual beliefs (thus in one coven a deist, a pantheist and an atheist can merry meet and conduct the rituals without much of a conflict). Nonetheless, some explanations can be made and in the following paper I would like to present images of the male deity of British Traditional Wicca, often recognised as "the Horned God." Referring to the writings of most Wiccan classical authors, prominent witches who have contributed to the development of this religion, I aim to provide an initial insight into a much broader and fascinating subject. I rely on sources written by representatives of both British Wiccan traditions, Gardnerian and Alexandrian: Gerald B. Gardner, without whom Wicca as we know it today would have never existed, Doreen Valiente, acknowledged as the mother of modern witchcraft, writer, poetess, occultist, and, last but not least, a Wiccan High Priestess and one of Gerald's Gardner most important working partners, Stewart and Jane Farrar, prolific Alexandrian witches,[6] and Wiccan High Priestess and Jungian psychologist Vivianne Crowley, who has explored both traditions. Those authors have been chosen due to their significant impact on the advance of British Traditional Wicca – as already stated, they are simply "classics." I will also draw from other Traditional Wiccan authors, like Morgana Sythove and Frederic Lamond. Works by witches representing other witchcraft traditions and solitary paths, among them Starhawk (Reclaiming tradition), Raymond Buckland (Saex Wicca) and Scott Cunningham (Solitary Wicca) will be introduced to provide a broader context.

Pagan witchcraft paths in the contemporary Western world are sometimes seen as related to the "Goddess movement." Indeed, some groups – like Dianic Wicca, established in the United States – exclude any male elements from their beliefs and practices, relating solely to the female aspect of the divine (which often results in forming women-only covens).[7] As Stewart Farrar notes, "if witches lean towards the Goddess, it is to redress the balance of contemporary civilization, which is heavily oriented towards the male principle (socially, theologically and psychically)."[8] However, in British Traditional Wicca, the polarity of male and

---

[6] The Farrars remain to be the most abundant source considering Alexandrian tradition, as Alex Sanders himself left scarce amount of writings.

[7] More on the emergence of Dianic traditions and Women's Mysteries – especially on Zsuzsanna Budapest, keen feminist – see C. Clifton, *Her Hidden Children*, pp. 120ff and M. Adler, *Drawing Down the Moon*, pp. 125-130.

[8] S. Farrar, *What Witches Do*, p. 22.

female is heavily stressed and both principles, though very much different from each other, are of equal importance. This polarity of male and female, of the God and the Goddess, has been underlined by many Wiccan authors, dating back to Gerald B. Gardner himself. In *The Meaning of Witchcraft* from 1959, he wrote:

> In a sense, the witch religion recognises all women as an incarnation of the Goddess, and all men as an incarnation of the God; and for this reason every woman is potentially a priestess, and every man potentially a priest; because to the witch the God and the Goddess are the Male and Female, the Right and the Left, the Two Pillars which support the Universe and every manifestation of male and female is a manifestation of Them.[9]

Gardner traces the origins of those deities as far as the Stone Ages, theorising on the myths of the Great Mother and god of death and hunting (which accords with the writings of Margaret Murray, namely, her witch-cult hypothesis described below). Scholar of contemporary Pagan studies Ethan Doyle White notes Gardner's patriotic tones in the description of the deities, especially when he writes about them as "the Ancient Ones of Britain, part of the land itself."[10]

A similar motif, the duotheistic approach, can be found in other analysed works. Vivianne Crowley acknowledges that while the emphasis on the God and the Goddess may differ in between various groups and localities, "Wicca believes that for wholeness the image of the Divine must contain both female and male," because worshipping only one divine aspect alone would "produce spiritual imbalance both for the individual and for society."[11] Janet and Stewart Farrar in the introduction to their *The Witches' God* explicitly admit:

> In the pagan cosmic view, the supreme creative polarity is that of the Goddess and God principles, for without polarity, from divinity downwards, there can be no manifestation (...). They are the two complementary terminals of the cosmic battery of all levels.[12]

---

9   G. B. Gardner, *The Meaning of Witchcraft*, p. 127.
10   Ibidem, p. 260. See also: E. Doyle White, op. cit., p. 88.
11   V. Crowley, *Phoenix from the Flame. Pagan Spirituality in Western World*, p. 103.
12   J. Farrar, S. Farrar, *The Witches' God* [www 03].

This complementarity of those two aspects resonates most strongly in British Traditional Wicca, obviously, yet it is also visible in the Pagan community in a more general sense. The British Pagan Federation, established in 1971 to inform the public about the Pagan worldview and to enable like-minded people to connect with one another, recognises three principles of membership. This triad embraces the general idea of what contemporary Paganism in Western world represents. Firstly, "Love for and Kinship with Nature," secondly, "A positive morality" often expressed as "Do what you will, as long as it harms none," and thirdly, "Recognition of the Divine, which transcends gender, acknowledging both the female and male aspect of Deity."[13] Those principles were first proposed by no one else but Doreen Valiente. In 1970, in a letter to John Score who announced the formation of Pagan Front (later to become Pagan Federation), Valiente exposed a "Pagan Creed," containing those three points. The last of them was "Love and kinship for nature – seen as interplay of complementary forces, which we symbolise as the Masculine and the Feminine, the Goddess and the God. The Horned God as the masculine side of Nature, the Moon Goddess as the feminine side."[14] Valiente compared this relationship to Chinese Yin and Yang and also to the Kabbalistic concept of Chokhmah and Binah on the Tree of Life.

The God and Goddess, therefore, are equally important in British Traditional Wicca and they cannot exist without each other. As put by Morgana, Gardnerian Wiccan High Priestess and Pagan Federation International coordinator, "in the Craft the Goddess does not stand alone. *She is the Giver of Form to the Formless Force whereby it can build*"[15] – the formless Force being, of course, the God. Similar thought can be found in Vivianne Crowley's works: she writes of the Divine as ultimately One, but within which the duality can be seen. Divine is the energy, she states, and energy is nothing but movement and change. "Where there is movement and change, there is action and reaction, passive and active, ebb and flow,"[16] and, consequently, male and female: namely, the God and the Goddess. "Without their creative difference, no current

---

[13]   *About the Pagan Federation* [www 01].
[14]   Underlined in the original version. The whole letter from Valiente to Score, see P. Heselton, *Doreen Valiente. Witch*, pp. 150-151.
[15]   Underlined in the original version. Morgana, *Beyond the Broomstick. Thoughts on the Philosophy of Wicca*, p. 47.
[16]   V. Crowley, *Phoenix from the Flame...*, p. 103.

flows,"[17] say the Farrars in aforementioned *The Witches' God*. This view can be found in the writings of other contemporary witches, not only those initiated into British Traditional Wicca. Starhawk, American witch, feminist, activist and founder of Reclaiming tradition, in her renowned book *The Spiral Dance* clearly states that "in most Witch traditions the God is seen as the other-half of the Goddess, and many of the rites and holiday are devoted to Him as well as to Her"[18] and characterises them both quite poetically, as following:

> The Goddess is the Encircler, the Ground of Being; the God is That-Which-Is-Brought-Forth, her mirror image, her other pole. She is the earth; He is the grain. She is the all-encompassing sky; He is the sun, her fireball. She is the Wheel; He is the Traveler. His is the sacrifice of life to death that life may go on. She is Mother and Destroyer; He is all that is born and is destroyed.[19]

In Aristotelian terms, the Goddess would be the matter, the God would represent the form and together they constitute one substance. Without the Goddess, there would be nothing to create from; without the God, there would be no impulse for any change to commence.

Polarity and complementarity aside: how can we interpret the male, the masculine, the God? Janet and Stewart Farrar briefly define the masculine principle as "the linear-logical, analysing, fertilizing aspect, with its emphasis on Ego-consciousness and individuality,"[20] whereas the Goddess, the feminine principle, would represent "the cyclical-intuitive, synthesizing, formative, nourishing aspect, with its emphasis on the riches of the Unconscious, both Personal and Collective, and on relatedness."[21] A more complex answer lies in the image of the God, recreated in rituals in the circle, repeated in the annual cycle of festivals, called the Wheel of the Year, which retells the story of God's rise, death and resurrection. Many modern Pagans, and Wiccans too, observe the cycle of eight main festivals, related to astronomical and agricultural

---

[17]   J. Farrar, S. Farrar, *The Witches' God* [www 03].
[18]   Starhawk, *Spiral Dance. A Rebirth of the Ancient Religions of the Great Goddess*, p. 121.
[19]   Ibidem, pp. 121-122.
[20]   J. Farrar, S. Farrar, *The Witches' God* [www 03].
[21]   Ibidem.

events. The Wheel of the Year nowadays consists of eight Sabbats, happening around every six weeks:

1. Yule (also known as the Winter Solstice) ..... circa 21st December
2. Imbolc (Oimelc or Candlemas)................ 2nd February
3. Spring Equinox (Ostara) .... circa 21st March
4. Beltane (May Eve)............................... 30th April
5. Summer Solstice (Midsummer, Litha) .... circa 21st June
6. Lammas (Lughnasad)............................ 1st August
7. Autumn Equinox (Mabon) .... circa 21st September
8. Samhain (Halloween)........................... 31st October[22]

This cycle reflects both the lifetime of the God and the changes of the seasons, that is, how the nature awakens during spring time, then blossoms and gives crops in late spring and summer, only to pass into darkness and hiding during the colder months. The God's own history in this cycle starts on Yule, when he is born from the Goddess, and therefore shares his birthday with celebrations of other holy beings, including Sol Invictus from the late Roman Empire and Jesus Christ.[23] From this cold night in midwinter the days grow longer and longer, as the God himself grows. In the beginning of February, with the coming of Imbolc, the God and Goddess return to this world from the Underworld; she becomes a young and beautiful virgin maiden again and is ready to mate with the God. They unite on the Spring Equinox, when the Goddess becomes pregnant, and celebrate their marriage on Beltane in the beginning of May, during a night full of love and passion. The peak of the God's power falls on the Summer Solstice, as he is acknowledged as the Lord and Consort of the Goddess and decides to sacrifice himself for his people. The sacrifice is fulfilled on Lammas, at the time of the harvest, when the God chooses to die for his people, fertilising the land – thus embodying

---

[22]   These dates are given by Doreen Valiente in *Witchcraft for Tomorrow*, p. 48, however, in other sources some festivals dates differ by a day or two. See e.g. J. Farrar, S. Farrar, *A Witches' Bible. The Complete Witches Handbook. Part 1: The Sabbats and Rites for Birth, Marriage and Death*. Other used names of the festivals are given in brackets.

[23]   Actually, the debate whether the date of Christmas was established purposely around the day of Sol Invictus has been ongoing for some time – see for example S. Hijmans, *Sol Invictus, the Winter Solstice, and the Origins of Christmas*.

the figure of the Dying God introduced by James Frazer.[24] He returns as conquering hero in the Autumn Equinox to take the Goddess back to the Underworld. On Samhain, the festival of the dead, the veil between this world and the other worlds is the thinnest, and as the autumn advances, the nights get longer and colder as the darkness seems to have overcome everything – but then, the beacon of hope is born on Yule yet again and the Wheel of the Year keeps on turning.[25]

This short outcome of the God's story in the cycle of the year already hints at the complexity of this figure. His connection with the Sun is not its only building component, since the God is also seen as the Lord of Death, Holly King and Oak King, and Green Man. "The God of witchcraft has always been problematic from a theological viewpoint,"[26] as bluntly stated by Janet Farrar and Gavin Bone. The God experiences successive stages of his life: as Vivianne Crowley notes, he is, accordingly, the Child of Promise, the Young Phallic God, the Green Man of Greendom and the Lover of the Goddess, the Sun King, the Sacrificial King, the leader of Heroic Quest and finally, the Dark Lord.[27] In the following paragraphs I discuss briefly four aspects by which he is known: the Lord of Death, the Oak and Holly King and the Green Man, and, firstly and most importantly, the Horned God.

This epithet – "Horned" – seems to be most common while addressing the Wiccan God, while the Goddess would be addressed as "the Triple Goddess," a threefold figure, symbolising three stages of womanhood – Maiden, Mother and Crone – associated with the phases of the Moon.[28]

---

[24] Frazer claims that the ancient people "again and again interpreted the dying and reviving god as the reaped and sprouted grain". J. Frazer, *The Golden Bough. A Study in Magic and Religion*, p. 392. Although the universality of the concept of the dying-and-rising god is debatable and has been both passionately rejected and strongly supported by various scholars, it still echoes in modern Paganism and witchcraft.

[25] This is a summary of the story given by V. Crowley, *Wicca...*, pp. 157-159. Similar one can be found in J. Farrar and S. Farrar, *A Witches' Bible. Part 1...*, pp. 25-27, although they include also the figures of Oak and Holly King (analysed further in the article). Academic analysis of the Wheel of the Year cycle, see J. Butler, *The Neo-Pagan Ritual Year*; E. Doyle White, op. cit., pp. 131-140.

[26] J. Farrar, G. Bone, *Progressive Witchcraft. Spirituality, Mysteries and Training in Modern Wicca*, p. 89.

[27] V. Crowley, *Wicca...*, p. 158.

[28] Interestingly, anthropologist Lynne Hume, based on her research in Australia, noted that some Wiccans also revere the God in his threefold form: the Youth, the Father, and the Wise Old Man, who reflect the life cycle of a man. See eadem, *Witchcraft and Paganism in Australia*.

So far, I have referred to both deities simply as "the God" and "the Goddess," but in British Traditional Wicca the God and Goddess have their own names, albeit mysterious ones. The names by which those two deities are invoked in rituals are supposed to be bound by the oath of secrecy; Wicca, as an initiatory and mystery religion, keeps most of the tradition handed down undisclosed. This does not mean that some content has not been published, on the contrary: many rituals and practices are thought to be generally revealed to the public and the books written by the Farrars can serve as a good example.[29] Leaving aside the question of secrecy, two names of the Horned God are known to the non-initiated: Karnayana and Cernunnos. According to Vivianne Crowley, the first name, preserved in Alexandrian Wicca, might refer to the Koranic portrayal of Alexander the Great, "Iskander Dh'l Karnain," meaning "Alexander the two-horned," as the king ordered to have him painted with two horns of Amoun, the Ram-God. In Gardnerian Wicca the name "Cernunnos" and sometimes "Herne" are used.[30] Cernunnos is the name conventionally applied to the Celtic horned deity and was found written on the so-called "Pillar of the Boatmen" from the 1st century CE, an altar from Roman Lutetia (today's Paris). The inscription, now worn away from time, was situated just above the bearded face with stag's antlers and two torcs hanging from them. Such a figure – with antlers, torcs, sometimes with legs crossed – appears also on the famous Gundestrup cauldron and other depictions. Judging from them, Phyllis Fray Bober reasons that Cernunnos represented "a god of fertility, not merely an abstract sense of flourishing nature, but also a specific reference to human fecundity and generation."[31] A stag, she adds, would pose as a most accurate symbol of the generative forces of nature and a man-like god figure with antlers may be an anthropomorphisation of an earlier animal divinity. The name itself probably means "the horned one", as proposed by 19th-century French scholars.[32]

Herne the Hunter, on the other hand, can boast of a less ancient origin. He entered the written history first in the Tudor period introduced

[29] The issue of secrecy in Wicca is very complex: see e.g. L. van Gulik, *Cleanliness is Next to Godliness, But Oaths are for Horses: Antecedents and Consequences of the Institutionalization of Secrecy in Initiatory Wicca*, pp. 233-255.

[30] V. Crowley, *Wicca...*,, p. 155. In case of the Goddess, Crowley gives the name "Aradia" as the most frequently used name in Wicca. Ibidem, p. 137.

[31] P. Fray Bober, *Cernunnos: Origin and Transformation of a Celtic Divinity*, p. 14.

[32] R. Hutton, *Pagan Britain*, p. 241.

by none other than William Shakespeare in his play *Merry Wives of Windsor*. According to the words of Mistress Page:

> There is an old tale goes that Herne the hunter,
> Sometime a keeper here in Windsor forest,
> Doth all the winter-time, at still midnight
> Walk round about an oak, with great ragg'd horns;
> And there he blasts the tree and takes the cattle
> And makes milch-kine yield blood and shakes a chain
> In a most hideous and dreadful manner.[33]

Horned, fearful, sending disease to cattle: hardly a pleasant figure. We cannot be sure whether this spirit was a pure Shakespearean invention or an adoption of an actual Windsor legend, still, Herne later has become quite successful as a local tourist attraction. In the middle of the 19th century he was transformed by popular novelist William Harrison Ainsworth to a spirit and protector of the Windsor Forest.[34] Local tradition was keen to accept Herne in his new role and this image – of a forest deity, more or less benevolent – has survived in a modern popular culture, including the *Robin of Sherwood* TV Series. Thus, historian Ronald Hutton describes Herne as "a literary figure whom modernity has back projected into the pagan past," although he considers his status of an actual, pre-Christian pagan god as doubtful.[35]

The main thread connecting those names and epithets – Horned, Karnayana, Cernunnos, Herne – seems to be hunting, woodlands and, more broadly, wild, pristine nature. This chant[36] by Kate West gathers all those themes together:

> Cernunnos, Horned One
> Cernunnos, King of the Sun

---

[33] W. Shakespeare, *The Merry Wives of Windsor*, Act IV, Scene 4 [www 5].
[34] Ainsworth has woven the figure of Herne the Hunter in the history of Henry VIII's pursuit of Anne Boleyn in his novel *Windsor Castle* (1843), and used a fragment of *The Merry Wives of Windsor* as an epigram for the novel. Idem, *Windsor Castle* [www 04].
[35] R. Hutton, *Pagan Britain…*, p. 381.
[36] Chants, popular in modern Pagan Witchcraft, consist of iterative verses and are used by the practitioners for example to raise the energy in the ritual circle. Many of them refer to the Goddess, like simple, but the famous one which is simply a list of names: "Isis, Astarte, Diana, Hecate, Demeter, Kali, Inanna."

Herne the Hunted and Hunter
Stag God of the Earth.[37]

In contemporary Paganism and modern Pagan witchcraft the turn to the reverence of nature and its cycles is a significant element of ritual practice and general worldview. The Horned God is "the force which greens the land,"[38] as put by Morgana. He is the one who recognises the greater good and is slain on Lammas for the sake of the land: "he accepts the inevitability of the ultimate sacrifice and is cut down by the Goddess,"[39] writes Vivianne Crowley. Once again, the sacrifice is the expression of God's vitality and fertility, also his sexuality and willingness to provide for his people.

It is worth noticing that in British Traditional Wicca, similarly as in many other contemporary witchcraft and Pagan traditions, the attitude to sexuality is positive and sex is perceived as a deep, holy experience. Gardner himself criticised the Christian approach to sexuality, especially the Church's accusations of witches being promiscuous. On the contrary, he noted, "witches do not believe in or encourage promiscuity. To them sex is something sacred and beautiful, which should not be allowed to become sordid or cheap."[40] The Farrars accordingly call sex an "unashamed and beautiful polarity-force which is intrinsic to the nature of the universe."[41] Scott Cunningham in his famous introduction to Eclectic Wicca for solitary practitioners speaks of the God as the one who, alongside with the Goddess, "celebrates and rules sex (...). The God lustily imbues us with the urge that ensures our species' biological future."[42] Sex, Cunningham adds, is a part of nature and is accepted as such and witches neither avoid it nor speak of it in hushed words. Because sex brings pleasure and prolongs the humans species, it should be treated as sacred. This sacredness can be seen in the Wiccan Great Rite,

[37] This chant can be found on CD *Elements of Chants*, released by a British Wiccan Kate West, initiated to Alexandrian tradition, and her coven, Hearth of Hecate [www 02].

[38] Morgana, op. cit., p. 47.

[39] V. Crowley, *Wicca...*, p. 164. In some covens, however, the God' death is ritually recreated on Midsummer, with the dominance of the Holly King over the Oak King – see J. Farrar, S. Farrar, *A Witches' Bible. Part 1...*, pp. 93–101 and further in this article.

[40] G. Gardner, *Meaning...*, p. 141. Further analysis of Gardner's view on sexuality, see e.g. J. Pearson, *Wicca and the Christian Heritage: Ritual, Sex and Magic*, pp. 81ff.

[41] J. Farrar, S. Farrar, *A Witches' Bible. Part 2: Principles, Rituals and Belief of Modern Witchcraft*, p. 32.

[42] S. Cunningham, *Wicca: A Guide for the Solitary Practitioner*, p. 13.

a ritual which embraces male-female polarity, performed as a form of sacred marriage – in most cases, only symbolically[43].

Back to the God's figure, the horns of the Horned One are those of a stag rather than any other animal, although sometimes the horns of a ram can be also encountered, like in the famous sculpture from the Museum of Witchcraft (Figure 1). The horns "reach up to heaven, capturing the power of the Sun and the stars,"[44] as poetically put by Vivianne Crowley. Horns may be treated as a visual manifestation of the God's strength and connection to nature. Naturally, the God of modern witches' is not the only deity in possession of horns and many such divine figures have been revered since ancient times. Actually, in analysed sources one can often encounter a thread connecting contemporary Wiccan Horned God with pre-Christian, even prehistoric times. One of the examples would be Gardner's aforementioned "the Ancient Ones of Britain," but Doreen Valiente also describes the deities of witches as "the oldest gods of all,"[45] referring to prehistoric carvings in Western Europe, which depict the horned god and naked goddess. She also mentioned Pan and Cernunnos as horned deities. Likewise, Vivianne Crowley explicitly refers to the Horned one God's "principal form that was worshipped by our earliest ancestors,"[46] giving a few famous representations from Palaeolithic Caves as an example, among them bison-headed man from La Pasiega in Spain and a man in antlers from the Cave of the Trois-Frères in France.[47]

Still, a certain supernatural being seems to have achieved quite a significant career in Western imagery, that is to say, the Christian Devil, the opponent of God, thought to be worshipped by witches during Sabbats in early modern Europe.[48] It would be impossible to retrace the

---

[43] The Great Rite, if actually performed, is conducted in private – in other cases it can be symbolised by uniting two objects representing the female or the Goddess and the male or the God, e.g. the chalice and athame, a ritual knife. See J. Farrar, S. Farrar, *A Witches' Bible. Part 1...*, pp. 48-54 and V. Crowley, *Wicca..*, pp. 221-222.

[44] V. Crowley, *Wicca...*, p. 156.

[45] D. Valiente, *Witchcraft...*, p. 23.

[46] V. Crowley, *Wicca...*, p. 154.

[47] The latter, sometimes called "The Sorcerer", has become known to public by sketches done by Henry Breuil in 1920s and more recent photographs give some doubts as to whether the figure had any horns at all. On those doubts see e.g. R. Hutton, *Witches, Druids and King Arthur*, pp. 33-35.

[48] The period of witch-hunt has been very deeply researched by many scholars, see for example R. Thurston, *The Witch Hunts: A History of the Witch Persecutions in Europe*

Figure 1. The Horned God statue in the Museum of Witchcraft and Magic
(Boscastle, Cornwall), photo: Joanna Malita-Król

exact origin of the connections between the image of the Christian Devil and the Horned God worshipped by witches in such a short article; still, those connections need to be highlighted, including the fact that it is generally agreed that the Devil's horns are an ancient pagan legacy.[49] The association of the horned deity and its witch-worshippers has been maintained up to modern times and one particular theory needs to be mentioned here: the witch-cult hypothesis, popularised by Margaret Alice Murray in her late works, with the controversial *The Witch-Cult in Western Europe* (1921) and *The God of the Witches* (1933). Murray basically tried to prove the existence of an early modern European witch religion, descended from antiquity, and the worship of a Horned God as the main principle of this cult.[50] Her thesis and the selective choice of source materials did not withstand the test of time nor critique and is not considered to be a reliable scientific theory.[51] It is also worth pointing out that contemporary witches seem to strongly oppose the idea of witches worshipping the Devil anytime. Gerald Gardner in *Witchcraft Today* openly mocked the idea of *osculum infame*, a charge commonly made during the witch-hunt period: "witches do not kiss the Devil's posterior, first because they never kiss anyone's posterior, and, secondly, because the Devil is never there for anyone to kiss."[52] This is the case of not only British Traditional Wicca: Reclaiming witch Starhawk states that "Witches do not believe in or worship the Devil – they consider it a concept peculiar to Christianity."[53]

It is also in the writings of Gerald Gardner where one can find the image of the witches' God as the Lord of Death and Resurrection. Yet again, he traces the origins of modern witches' gods back to prehistorical times – when women acted as priestesses for the Great Mother Goddess, while men revered a hunting god, who also went on to rule the beyond,

---

and North America.

[49] On the resemblance between the Christian Devil and ancient pagan gods, see e.g. B. Levack, *The Witch-Hunt in Early Modern Europe*, pp. 33-34.

[50] "I have traced the worship of the Horned God onwards through the centuries from the Palaeolithic prototypes and I have shown that the survival of the cult was due to the survival of the races who adored the god", as M. Murray writes in the introduction to *The God of the Witches*, p. 14.

[51] More on Murray's thesis and its critics, see for example R. Hutton, *The Triumph...*, pp. 194-201.

[52] G. B. Gardner, *Witchcraft Today*, p. 112.

[53] Starhawk, op. cit., p. 120.

a kind of paradise. This concept has survived throughout the centuries and Gardner's fellow witches also recognised the God as Death:

> My witches speak of him as god of "Death and what lies beyond": by this they not only mean the life in the next world but resurrection (or reincarnation). He rules a sort of happy hunting ground, where ordinary folk go and forgather with like-minded people.[54]

This means, Gardner elaborates, that the worshippers of this particular god will meet in a "special paradise" and then be reborn in the same tribe – or, nowadays, a witch circle.[55] What is more, there is one particular story which features the God as the Lord of Death, the *Legend of the Descent*, retold by Gardner in *Witchcraft Today*. It is the story of the Goddess (respectfully called "G.") who "journeyed to the nether lands,"[56] obediently tackling all the challenges lying along the way. Gardner describes the two deities as they finally unite in love and passion: G. and Death, the lord of the nether lands, who teaches G. all the mysteries. The Goddess, first reluctant and unconvinced by Death's proclamations of love and devotion, finally yields to him, "for each without the other will bring misery and destruction,"[57] Gardner also describes the nature of enacting this story: when the priestess[58] impersonates the Goddess in the ritual, she communes with her and, accordingly, the priest who impersonates the God "becomes at one with him in his aspect of Death, the Consoler, the Comforter, the bringer of a happy after-life and regeneration. The initiate in undergoing the god's experiences becomes a witch."[59] The legend is enacted at the end of the ritual of second degree initiation, when the initiated person is given the title of High Priest or

---

[54] G. B. Gardner, *Witchcraft Today*, p. 32. In this very book Gardner reported the views of the witches from the New Forest coven, which may be called a proto-Wiccan coven. About this gathering and the debate on its actual existence, see e.g. E. Doyle White, op. cit. pp. 25-28.

[55] The reincarnation is, according to Ethan Doyle White, "dominant afterlife belief in Wicca", although not every practitioner accepts it. E. Doyle White, op. cit., pp. 146ff.

[56] G. B. Gardner, *Witchcraft Today*, p. 41.

[57] V. Crowley, *Wicca…*, pp. 204-205.

[58] In British Traditional Wicca, every initiate during the ritual of first degree initiation is bestowed with the title "the priestess and witch" or "the priest and witch".

[59] G. B. Gardner, *Witchcraft Today*, p. 145.

High Priestess along with the authority to transmit the tradition and initiate new witches to the first degree.[60]

The ritual encounter with the God as the Dark Lord, the Lord of Death, may seem a particularly fearful experience, yet Vivianne Crowley cautions against misunderstanding and treating the Dark Lord as a malevolent figure. "The Dark Lord in Wicca," she writes, "is not evil. He is the Lord of the Underworld, the kingdom of the unconscious mind, and in identifying with him a male initiate discovers the Dark Lord's true nature."[61] By acknowledging the natural law of death, the Goddess in the legend understands the inevitability of passing, but she also discovers the mystery of rebirth. According to Crowley, an initiate during the ritual of second initiation encounters Jungian Shadow, meeting with his or her contra-sexual side.[62] This again underlines the importance of polarity of the male and female principle in British Traditional Wicca.

We have already observed how the Wheel of the Year reflects the story of the God, who rises and falls with the Sun, yet it is only one of two themes, visible in the yearly cycle. The second one, the natural-fertility theme, involves two God-figures: the Oak King and the Holly King. These two divine representations refer to the year being divided into two parts: the winter half, which is the Waning Year, beginning on the Autumn Equinox, and peaking at Midwinter, ruled by the Holly King; and the summer half, the Waxing Year, beginning on the Spring Equinox and peaking at Midsummer, ruled by the Oak King. They are complementary twin brothers, eternally competing, eternally prevailing and succeeding one after the other. Both of them strive to win the favour of the Goddess and, as put by the Farrars, "each at the peak of his half-yearly reign, is sacrificially mated with her dies in her embrace and is resurrected to complete his reign."[63] Although they represent the light and the dark, again, it does not mean one of them is good and the other one is evil. Once more, the polarity of two complementary forces and the creative tension between them should be stressed here.

---

[60]   There are three degrees of initiation in British Traditional Wicca, with a preliminary rank of "neophyte" in some Alexandrian covens. For the rite of second degree initiation, see J. Farrar, S. Farrar, *A Witches' Bible. Part 2...*, pp. 21-30.

[61]   V. Crowley, *Wicca...*, p. 202.

[62]   "For a woman, this is a meeting with her Animus and for a man a meeting with his Anima". Ibidem, p. 205.

[63]   J. Farrar, S. Farrar, *A Witches' Bible. Part 1...*, p. 24.

The idea of two counter figures, battling through the yearly cycle, has been suggested also by James Frazer in *Golden Bough* and Robert Graves in *White Goddess*. Frazer refers to folk customs, appearing throughout Europe: a "dramatic contest between actors who play the part respectively of Winter and Summer,"[64] whereas Graves in his description of myth-making quotes several poems and stories which would represent the struggle between Oak and Holly, for example, Irish version of *Romance of Gawain and the Green Knight*.[65] One could wonder how the two brothers relate to the previously described Sun God in a witchcraft and Pagan context. The Farrars suggest, if one should find the transition from the Horned God to the two Kings problematic, that the Oak and Holly Kings can be treated as "a subtlety which developed in amplification of the Horned God concept as vegetation became more important to man."[66] This means the Horned One would be related more closely to the woods and hunting, and the two divine twins to agriculture.

One more image needs to be briefly mentioned, namely the Green Man. A foliate male face can be found carved as a part of church ornaments since the twelfth century, mostly in Britain, but also in France and Germany. Some scholars have recognised it as a representation of a pagan i.e. pre-Christian deity[67] and the first to do so was Lady Raglan of the British Folklore Society. She was also the one to apply the name "the Green Man" to this type of the image, believing it to be connected to a Pagan fertility god, maybe even a descendant of the myth of Odin or of Attis.[68] Nowadays the tendency is not to give any ultimate interpretation of the Green Man church ornaments, as we cannot be certain what they meant to its creators. However, some authors are still inclined to interpret the foliate face on churches as a reminiscence of the Pagan past. For example, Gardnerian Wiccan and founder of Seax-Wica tradition Raymond Buckland in *The Witch Book* explicitly writes about artisans, who followed "the Old Religion" in Christian times and incorporated images of their own gods. "These figures," describes Buckland, "carved in wood and stone, were of the god of nature, his face surrounded by

---

[64] J. Frazer, op. cit., p. 367.
[65] R. Graves, *The White Goddess*, pp. 179-180
[66] J. Farrar, S. Farrar, *A Witches' Bible. Part 1...*, p. 24.
[67] See R. Hutton, *Pagan Britain*, pp. 347-350.
[68] She explicitly refers to James G. Frazer on this matter. See Lady Raglan, *The "Green Man" in Church Architecture*, p. 54.

leaves, fruit and nuts."[69] Religious studies scholar Joanne Pearson presents the Green Man as "regarded as a blatantly Pagan image"[70] and indeed, he has found his place in modern Paganism too. The Farrars consider the aforementioned Oak King "doubtless relatable" to the Green Man[71] and for them this once again represents the male aspect's connection to nature. The image of the Green Man can be used nowadays as a decorative ornament (see Figure 2), and, referring anew to Pearson, the name itself "has long been a popular name for that most sacred of Pagan places, the pub!"[72]

This short insight into various aspects of the Wiccan God shows that he can be revered in many forms, suitable to the time of the year, but also the coven or witch's preferences. Establishing a relationship with the God and Goddess, no matter how they are understood, and worshipping them in rituals remains one of the crucial elements of practise in British Traditional Witchcraft.[73] Proper rituals, performed during Wheel of the Year's Sabbats and on other occasions,[74] can provide one way of devotion, but a more private relationship can also be formed, according to practitioners' personal tastes and needs. Frederick Lamond, Gardnerian Wiccan and a member of Bricket Wood coven,[75] makes an interesting observation in this matter: the Horned God icon does not speak to modern people as strongly as the Goddess and ceased to be a role model, because the role of men as breadwinners has changed throughout the millennia. "Few of us are hunters any more: we earn our livings as engineers, computer programmers and operators, managers, salesman (…) in our highly complex industrial civilisation, and to these modern tasks the Horned God has little to say,"[76] he writes, once again referring to the ancient origin of the God, also mentioned in other analysed sources. Nowadays, Lamond points out, the mighty hunter-god figure remains less the professional inspiration and more of a representation of

---

[69]   R. Buckland, *The Witch Book*, p. 182.
[70]   J. Pearson, *A Popular Dictionary of Paganism*, p. 72.
[71]   J. Farrar, S. Farrar, *A Witches' Bible. Part 1…*, p. 24.
[72]   J. Pearson, *A Popular Dictionary…*, p. 72.
[73]   On the mystical aspect of Wicca see V. Crowley, *Wicca as Modern-day Mystery Religion*.
[74]   Other occasions include the esbats, coven meetings other than Sabbats, during which the Gods can be also invited to the ritual circle. See for example J. Farrar, S. Farrar, *A Witches' Bible. Part 1…*, pp. 28ff and for more eclectic view R. Buckland, *The Witch Book*, p. 159.
[75]   First coven established by Gardner, i.e. the first coven in Gardnerian line.
[76]   F. Lamond, *Fifty Years of Wicca*, pp. 109-110.

Figure 2. Modern rendition of the Green Man, photo: Joanna Malita-Król

the male lust, a good role model for men to "overcome our sexual inhibitions."[77] Still, a certain relationship can be established, and God's role in the Wheel of the Year's rituals remains of great importance.

Coming back to the question previously asked: what does it mean, the male, the masculine, the God? A look at him as a Horned One, the Oak and Holly King, the Green Man and the Lord of Death provides us with a few threads which contribute to a better understanding of the male divinity of British Traditional Wicca. He is "the active, fertilizing

[77]   Ibidem, p. 110.

energetic, pursuing principle," compared to "the passive, fertile, gestating, nourishing" divine female, as put by Stewart Farrar.[78] While sometimes the God might seem to be overwhelmed by the Goddess, he remains to be equally significant. The two divine principles, male and female, cannot exist without each other, as they are thought to be complementary, neither being superior to the other one. Morgana calls it the "dual godhead", adding that "their union is the power of the universe."[79] The God is represented by the Sun and his life journey of the Wheel of the Year, from birth in winter to retirement to the Underworld in autumn, reflecting the journey of the Sun in the course of the astronomical year. Strongly connected to sexuality and energy, the God is the patron of animals, woodland and hunting, likewise the patron of what grows and is harvested. Recognising the needs of his people, the God offers himself to be slain, fertilising the land. His horns symbolise the connection to nature, his strength and vitality. As the Lord of Darkness he is "the Consoler, the Comforter," representing the destructive force which is indispensable for the balance of the universe.

BIBLIOGRAPHY

About the Pagan Federation [www 01].
Adler M., *Drawing Down the Moon: Witches, Druids, Goddess-Worshippers, and Other Pagans in America Today*, Penguin/Arkana, New York 2006.
Ainsworth W. H., *Windsor Castle*, 1843 [www 04].
Buckland R., *Witch Book: The Encyclopedia of Witchcraft, Wicca, and Neo-Paganism,* Visible Ink Press, Canton 2001.
Butler J., *The Neo-Pagan Ritual Year*, "Cosmos", Vol. 18, 2002, pp. 121-142.
Clifton C., *Her Hidden Children. The Rise of Wicca and Paganism in America*, Altamira Press, Lanham 2006.
Crowley V., *Phoenix from the Flame. Pagan Spirituality in the Western World*, The Aquarian Press, London 1994.
Crowley V., *Wicca as Modern-day Mystery Religion* [in:] *Pagan Pathways. A Guide to the Ancient Earth Traditions*, G. Harvey, C. Hardman (ed.), Thorsons, London 2000, pp. 81-93.
Crowley V., *Wicca. A Comprehensive Guide to the Old Religion in the Modern World*, Element, London 2003.
Cunningham S., *Wicca: A Guide for the Solitary Practitioner*, Llewellyn Publications, Woodbury 2007.
Doyle White E., *Wicca. History, Belief, and Community in Modern Pagan Witchcraft*, Sussex Academic Press, Brighton-Portland-Toronto 2016.

[78] S. Farrar, *What Witches Do*, p. 22.
[79] Morgana, op. cit., p. 14.

Element of Chants [www 02].

Farrar S., *What Witches Do*, Robert Hale, London 1995.

Farrar J., Bone G., *Progressive Witchcraft. Spirituality, Mysteries and Training in Modern Wicca*, New Page Books, Franklin Lakes 2004.

Farrar J., Farrar S., *A Witches' Bible. The Complete Witches Handbook. Part 1: The Sabbats and Rites for Birth, Marriage and Death. Part 2: Principles, Rituals and Belief of Modern Witchcraft*, Robert Hale Limited, Marlborough 1997.

Farrar J., Farrar S., *The Witches' God*, David & Charles, 2012 (no place of publication) [www 03].

Fortune D., *The Sea Priestess*, Samuel Weiser Inc., York Beach 1985.

Fray Bober P., *Cernunnos: Origin and Transformation of a Celtic Divinity*, "American Journal of Archaeology", Vol. 55, No. 1, 1951, pp. 13–51.

Frazer J., *The Golden Bough. A Study in Magic and Religion*, Touchstone, New York 1995.

Gardner G. B., *Meaning of Witchcraft*, Magickal Childe, New York 1982.

Gardner G. B., *Witchcraft Today*, Citadel Press, New York 2004.

R. Graves, *The White Goddess: A Historical Grammar of Poetic Myth*, Farrar, Straus and Giroux, New York 1966.

Gulik van L., *Cleanliness is Next to Godliness, But Oaths are for Horses: Antecedents and Consequences of the Institutionalization of Secrecy in Initiatory Wicca*, "Pomegranate. The International Journal of Pagan Studies", Vol. 12, 2012, pp. 233–255.

Heselton P., *Doreen Valiente. Witch*, The Doreen Valiente Foundation and The Centre For Pagan Studies, 2016 (no place of publication).

Heselton P., *Wiccan Roots: Gerald Gardner and the Modern Witchcraft Revival*, Capall Bann Publishing, Chieveley 2000.

Hijmans S., *Sol Invictus, the Winter Solstice, and the Origins of Christmas*, "Mouseion", Vol. 47, No. 3, 2003, pp. 277–298.

Hume L., *Witchcraft and Paganism in Australia*, Melbourne University Press, Carlton South 1997.

Hutton R., *Pagan Britain*, Yale University Press, New Haven-London 2014.

Hutton R., *The Triumph of the Moon. A History of Modern Pagan Witchcraft*, Oxford University Press, Oxford 2010.

Hutton R., *Witches, Druids and King Arthur*, Hambledon Continuum, London 2006.

Lamond F., *Fifty Years of Wicca*, Green Magic, Long Barn 2004.

Levack B., *The Witch-Hunt in Early Modern Europe*, Routledge, London-New York, 2013.

Morgana, *Beyond the Broomstick. Thoughts on the Philosophy of Wicca*, Whyte Tracks, Copenhagen 2008.

Murray M., *The God of the Witches*, Oxford University Press, Oxford 1970.

Pearson J., *A Popular Dictionary of Paganism*, Routledge, London-New York 2013 (e-book version).

Pearson J., *Wicca and the Christian Heritage: Ritual, Sex and Magic*, Routledge, London and New York 2007.

Raglan L., *The "Green Man" in Church Architecture*, "Folklore", Vol. 50, No. 1, 1959, pp. 54–57.

Starhawk, *The Spiral Dance. A Rebirth of the Ancient Religions of the Great Goddess*, Harper Collins, New York 1999.

Thurston R., *The Witch Hunts: A History of the Witch Persecutions in Europe and North America*, Routledge, New York 2013.

Valiente D., *The Rebirth of Witchcraft*, Phoenix Publishing Inc., Custer 1989.

Valiente D., *Witchcraft for Tomorrow*, Robert Hale, Marlborough 2016.

Internet sources used

[www 01] http://www.paganfederation.org/about-the-pf/#Principles (accessed: 25.10.2017)

[www 02] http://kate-west.webs.com/music.htm (accessed: 31.10.2017)

[www 03] https://books.google.pl/books?id=oqHn8mXWT8QC&printsec=frontcover&hl=pl#v=onepage&q&f=false (accessed: 30.10.2017)

[www 04] http://www.gutenberg.org/files/2866/2866-h/2866-h.htm (accessed: 06.04.2018)

[www 05] https://gutenberg.org/files/1517/1517-h/1517-h.htm#A3S4 (accessed: 03.08.2021)

Figures

Figure 1. The Horned God statue in the Museum of Witchcraft and Magic (Boscastle, Cornwall; the authorship of the statue was not indicated on the exhibition), photo: Joanna Malita-Król (taken on 21.02.2017)

Figure 2. Modern rendition of the Green Man (from "The Goddess & The Green Man" shop in Glastonbury, 17 High Street), photo: Joanna Malita-Król (taken on 18.02.2017)

BIOGRAPHICAL NOTES OF THE AUTHORS

KATARZYNA BORKOWSKA, MA, assistant at the L.&A. Birkenmajer Institute for the History of Science, PAS; PhD student in Classics at Institute of Classics, University of Warsaw. Working on a PhD on Cicero's translations and paraphrases of Plato. Research interests include ancient philosophy and the history of ideas. Her PhD dissertation will have the title *Cyceron i Platon: tłumaczenia, parafrazy, nawiązania* under the guidance of Prof. dr. hab. Mikołaj Szymański. Her main interests are history and evolution of ideas. E-mail: kasia.bor@gmail.com

AGNIESZKA GONDOR-WIERCIOCH works as an adjunct at the Institute of American Studies and Polish Diaspora on the Jagiellonian University. Her PhD, defended at the Faculty of Philology, was published as the book *Dwa światy, dwie pamięci – dylemat wielokulturowości w wybranych utworach Louise Erdrich i José Maríi Arguedasa* in 2009. Awarded the stipend of JFK Institute in Berlin in 2013. She teaches about Latin-American literature, as well as American and Canadian literature. Her research deals with comparative analysis of ethnic literatures in the USA, connections between American and Latin-American literature, transcultural processes, and heterogenic discourse. Her latest book is called *Pomiędzy rekonstrukcją a mitem. Role historii we*

współczesnej prozie rdzennych Amerykanów i Latino (2016).
E-mail: agnieszka.gondor-wiercioch@uj.edu.pl

KHALIL A. ARAB – Iranist, a PhD student at the Faculty of Philology
of the Jagiellonian University, Kraków, Poland. He is currently preparing a doctoral dissertation on the relationship
between humans and animals in modern Dari-language
Afghan literature.

MATEUSZ M. KŁAGISZ – PhD in Iranian studies, works in the
Institute of Oriental Studies at the Jagiellonian University, Kraków, Poland. He is currently preparing a mon-
ograph devoted to the Pashtun *landays*, i.e. folk couplets,
supplemented with their translations into Polish. E-mail:
mateusz.klagisz@uj.edu.pl

ANNA KUCHTA, PhD, is a graduate of the Centre for Comparative
Studies of Civilizations (Jagiellonian University in Kraków,
Poland), where she currently works as a lecturer and researcher. She is a recipient of The Ryoichi Sasakawa Young
Leaders Fellowship which resulted in a research project
concerning Japanese literature at Kobe University (Japan)
in May 2016. In July 2019 she defended with honors her
doctoral thesis focusing on postmemory in Polish contemporary literature. Her main research interests include
postmemory, trauma and its transmission and tracing
relations between literature and popular culture. She is a
member of "The Polish Journal of Aesthetics" and "The
Polish Journal of the Arts and Culture. New Series" editorial boards. E-mail: anna.kuchta@uj.edu.pl

KWASU DAVID TEMBO is a PhD graduate from the University of
Edinburgh's Language, Literatures, and Cultures department. His research interests include comics studies, literary theory and criticism, and philosophy. He has published widely in these areas in journals and chapters across
the world. E-mail: tembo.kwasu@gmail.com. Affiliation:
independent researcher.

RENATA IWICKA holds her PhD in cultural studies after completing her master's degree in Japanese Studies (Faculty of Oriental Philology, Jagiellonian University). Her main area of research is Japanese nationalism, popculture and Korean culture. E-mail: renata.iwicka@uj.edu.pl

JOANNA MALITA-KRÓL is a researcher and lecturer in cultural and religious studies at the Institute for the Study of Religions, Jagiellonian University. She is also a JASSO stipend holder (Kobe University). In March 2019 she defended her doctoral thesis dedicated to the Polish Traditional Wiccan *milieu*, entitled *Polish Wiccans. A Study of Lived Religion*. Her academic interests centre around contemporary witchcraft and Paganism, yet she also explores Japanese culture, especially the Heian period with *The Tale of Genji*. E-mail: j.malita-krol@uj.edu.pl. Affiliation: Institute for the Study of Religions, Jagiellonian University.

KSENIA OLKUSZ is a literary historian, critic, and theorist; she is professor at the head of Facta Ficta Research Centre in Wrocław as well as editor-in-chief of open access "Facta Ficta. Journal of Theory, Narrative & Media" (factafictajournal.com); she has authored books *Współczesność w zwierciadle horroru. O najnowszej polskiej literaturze grozy* (2010) and *Materializm kontra ezoteryka: drugie pokolenie pozytywistów wobec "spraw nie z tego świata"* (2017), *Narracje zombiecentryczne. Teoria – Antropologia –Literatura* (2019) as well as edited volumes *Zombie w kulturze* (2016) and *Światy grozy* (2016), *Narracje fantastyczne* (2017), *Rejestry kultury* (2019) and also *More After More. Essays Commemorating the Five-Hundredth Anniversary of Thomas More's Utopia* (2016); since 2016 she has been also the leading editor of the series "Perspektywy Ponowoczesności" and supervisor of all Facta Ficta Research Centre publishing projects; her research interests span across popular culture, postclassical narratology, literature studies, dystopian studies, horror, gothic, and crime fiction. E-mail: xenia.olkusz@gmail.com

Editor
Renata Włodek

Proofreader
Małgorzata Szul

Typesetter
Paweł Noszkiewicz

Jagiellonian University Press
Editorial Offices: Michałowskiego St. 9/2, 31-126 Krakow
Phone: +48 12 663 23 80

GPSR Authorized Representative: Easy Access System Europe, Mustamäe tee 50, 10621 Tallinn, Estonia, gpsr.requests@easproject.com